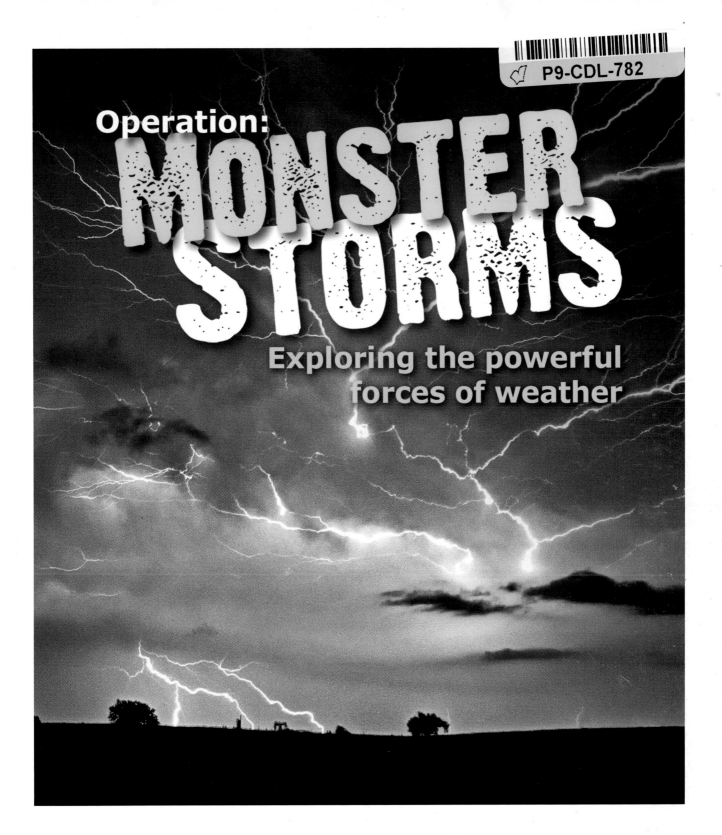

Operation: MONSTER STORMS

Exploring the powerful forces of weather

NATIONAL GEOGRAPHIC

The JAS⦿N Project

A nonprofit subsidiary of the National Geographic Society, The JASON Project connects students with great explorers and great events to inspire and motivate them to learn science. JASON works with the National Aeronautics and Space Administration (NASA), the National Oceanic and Atmospheric Administration (NOAA) and the National Geographic Society to develop multimedia science curricula based on their cutting-edge missions of exploration and discovery. By providing educators with those same inspirational experiences—and giving them the tools and resources to improve science teaching—JASON seeks to reenergize them for a lasting, positive impact on students.

To learn more about The JASON Project and new things happening at JASON, visit us online at
www.jason.org

E-mail us at *info@jason.org*

Cover Design: Mazer Creative Services

Cover Images

Main cover and title page: Dramatic cloud-to-cloud lightning in the night sky east of Norman, Oklahoma on July 7, 1994. Photo by Weatherpix Stock Images.

Front cover thumbnails: (left) Student Argonaut Matthew Worsham taking wind data measurements with Host Researcher Shirley Murillo. Photo by Peter Haydock, The JASON Project; (right) Student Argonaut Jing Fan in the field with Host Researcher Tim Samaras. Photo by Jude Kesl.

Back cover thumbnails: (top left) Student Argonaut Neil Muir gets a close-up look at Aerosonde before launch. Photo by Peter Haydock, The JASON Project; (top right) Student Argonauts Matthew Worsham and Cassandra Santamaria from Missions 4 and 5. Photo by Jude Kesl; (middle left) Cassandra Santamaria works with Host Researcher Shirley Murillo. Photo by Jude Kesl; (lower right) Hurricane Katrina located south-southeast of Louisiana on August 28, 2005. Photo by NOAA; Tornado photo courtesy of Tim Samaras.

Published by The JASON Project.

The JASON Project
Permissions Requests
44983 Knoll Square
Ashburn, VA 20147

Phone: 888-527-6600
Fax: 877-370-8988

ISBN 978-0-9787574-0-3

Printed in the United States of America
by the Courier Companies, Inc.

10 9 8 7 6 5 4

National Geographic and the Yellow Border are trademarks of the National Geographic Society.

Contents

Scientific Visualization Studio, NASA/GSFC

Getting Started with *Operation: Monster Storms*

Developed in collaboration with our partners at National Geographic, NASA, and NOAA, *Operation: Monster Storms* is built on a Mission framework to capture the energy and excitement of authentic exploration and discovery. The *Operation* consists of five captivating Missions that provide the real-world challenges, the science background knowledge, and the tools to help you solve each mission challenge.

Let's take a closer look at the parts of each Mission!

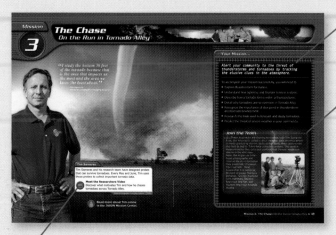

Mission Objectives

Each Mission will start with a list of objectives that you will find on this opening page.

Meet The Team

Your Mission begins with an invitation to the join the Host Researcher and Argonaut team. You will work side-by-side with this team as they guide you through your study of atmospheric conditions, storm formation, hurricanes, tornadoes, and emergency preparation and response.

Video and Online Resources

You will also see icons directing you to the Host Researcher video where you will get to know more about the Mission team leader. Keep watch for these icons and others. They will indicate when you will find multimedia resources online in the **JASON Mission Center.**

Introduction Article

Once you have your objectives and have met the team, each new Mission will introduce you to a day in the life of the Host Researcher, and the unique work that brings this scientist face-to-face with monster weather.

Feel the roller coaster ride as a NOAA hurricane hunter aircraft flies through a hurricane, or scramble to set out data collection probes as a tornado comes barreling ever-closer toward you!

Mission Briefing Videos

See these adventures come alive in every Mission Briefing Video, which gives an action-packed introduction to the Mission objectives and key science concepts.

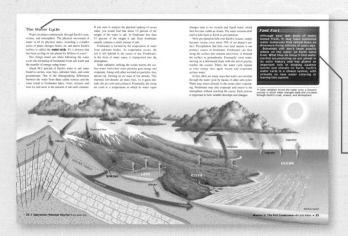

Briefing Articles

Gather all of your background information and clues through a series of Mission Briefing articles that guide you through the science of monster weather so that you can complete your Mission objectives.

Full-color graphics enhance the description and explanation of essential science concepts so that you can clearly see the ideas presented in the briefings.

Fast Fact

You'll find interesting things you've never thought of before in *Fast Facts*. Could the last glass of water you drank actually have contained water molecules that rained down on a *Tyrannosaurus* millions of years ago? Find out on page 33.

Team Highlights

Get an up-close view of the investigations that our Host Researchers and Argonauts have conducted during their field work for *Operation: Monster Storms*.

Researcher Tools

Check out the amazing tools that researchers use during their explorations in the field. From uninhabited aerial vehicles to data-gathering probes, you'll learn how these tools help researchers unlock the secrets of monster storms.

Mission Labs

Put your knowledge to work with several hands-on labs in each Mission. The labs provide opportunities to practice and refine the skills you need in order to complete your mission objectives. In these labs, you'll build weather tools, conduct experiments, collect data, and describe your observations and conclusions in your JASON Journal.

Digital Labs

Visit the **JASON Mission Center** for an interactive adventure in Digital Labs such as *Storm Tracker*. You can try your hand at these interactive simulations, and take the challenge of tracking and confronting real monster weather.

Additional Online Resources

You'll find other great resources in the **JASON Mission Center** too, including your JASON Journal. Use it to record your work and experiences as you complete your *Operation: Monster Storms* Missions. Check the JASON Home Page often for podcasts and Webcasts that will provide updates on your Mission and on other breaking news in science.

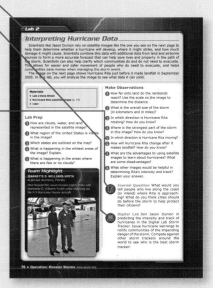

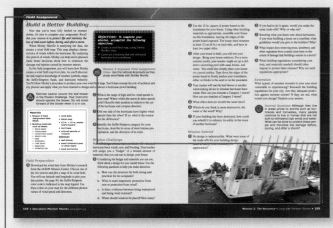

Connections

Learn to look for and find the amazing connections between science concepts and other things that you experience in the world around you. *Connections* features highlight thought-provoking links that you can uncover between science and human culture, history, geography, math, literature, strange phenomena, and other interesting topics.

Field Assignments

Field Assignments at the conclusion of each Mission give you the opportunity to put your new science skills and ideas to work in the field. To complete your Mission, you will need to accomplish the objectives set out in a Mission Challenge, then provide an analysis during your Mission Debrief.

Argonaut Videos, Journals, and Photo Galleries

Argonaut Field Assignment Videos let you join the Argo team as they conduct their field work for selected Missions at Wallops Island, Virginia, outside Denver, Colorado, and in Miami, Florida. Login to the **JASON Mission Center** to read the Argonaut journals and take a look at their photo galleries documenting their field experience!

Your Tour of the JASON Mission Center

The **JASON Mission Center (JMC)** is your online hub for *Operation: Monster Storms* content and resources and for the Argonaut community. Your JASON experience will come to life through inter-active games, Digital Labs, video segments, your own JASON Journals, and other community resources and tools that support the Missions in this book.

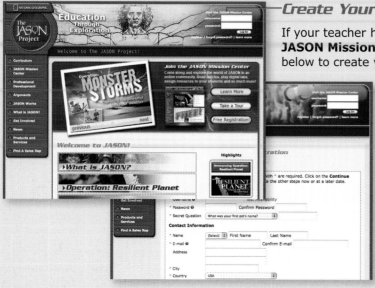

Create Your Own Free Student Account

If your teacher has made an account for you, simply login to the **JASON Mission Center.** Otherwise, follow these simple steps below to create your own account.

1. Go to *www.jason.org*
2. Look for the **JASON Mission Center** in the upper right.
3. Click "Register."
4. Choose "Student" as your role –*OR*– if your teacher provided you with a class-room code, enter it now.
5. Enter your email address or your guardian's email address and select a password for your account that you can easily remember.

The JASON Mission Center Home Page

Welcome to your **JASON Mission Center** home page. From here you can quickly access all the wonderful JASON tools and resources as you begin your Mission. Take a moment to read the latest JASON news, try a search of the Digital Library, or jump right into *Operation: Monster Storms* on the Web!

Here are some of the things you'll see . . .

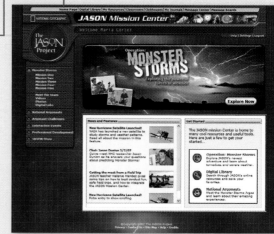

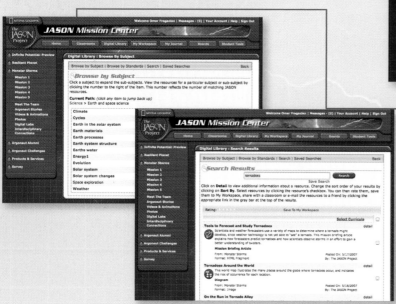

Your Resources and Tools

Powerful online tools are always at your fingertips. Use the *Digital Library* to find any JASON resource quickly and easily. Save and organize your favorites in *My Resources*. View assignments and community updates in your *Classrooms* menu. These resources and more are always accessible through the tools menu at the top of the **JASON Mission Center** page.

My Journal and Other Community Tools

Your student account on **JMC** includes a private online JASON Journal that allows you take notes, write about what you have learned, and respond to Journal Questions during the Missions. Other Community Tools include a moderated message board, classroom home pages, and tools to communicate with JASON researchers about their ongoing work in the field.

Online Version of Operation: Monster Storms

This entire student edition book is also available to you online, for easy access anytime, anywhere. You can view, download, and print any page from any Mission.

Team Info, Videos, and Photo Galleries

Learn more about the Host Researchers and the Argonauts from their biographies and journals. Video segments feature the Mission teams in action. Photo galleries provide additional views of the researchers and Argonauts at work, as well as stunning collections of more monster storm images.

Digital Labs

The Digital Lab *StormTracker* puts you in the role of a hurricane researcher. Can *you* predict where the storm will go, how strong it will be, and whether it will threaten cities? Host Researcher Jason Dunion comes along for the ride to help you make the right call! *StormTracker* plus several mini-labs are available in the Digital Labs section of the JMC.

Argonaut Resources

The Argonaut Challenge provides you and every other Argonaut a chance to complete a multimedia project that you can share online with the entire JASON community. You can also visit the message boards to discuss JASON with other local and National Argonauts around the world.

Your Mission begins at *www.jason.org*

Profiling the Suspects
Trouble Brewing in Earth's Atmosphere

"If we better understand monster storms, we will ultimately save lives and property."

—Anthony Guillory
Airborne Science Manager, NASA

Anthony Guillory

Anthony Guillory uses an uninhabited aerial vehicle (UAV), a large remotely controlled airplane, to study tropical storms and hurricanes. The aircraft is launched from the roof of a moving truck.

Meet the Researchers Video
Witness NASA's newest probe in use, gathering the best data on hurricanes and other weather events.

Airborne Science Manager, NASA

Read more about Anthony online in the JASON Mission Center.

Photos above (left to right): NASA; NOAA Photo Library/National Severe Storms Laboratory (NSSL); Peter Haydock, The JASON Project; Marvin Nauman, FEMA Photo

Your Mission...

Gather critical weather intelligence for your community so that you can anticipate the threat of a monster storm.

To accomplish your mission successfully, you will need to

- Define a storm and other extreme weather events.
- Understand how energy gets from the Sun to Earth.
- Recognize the difference between the greenhouse effect and global warming.
- Identify the components of air and understand how air pressure changes.
- Explain how wind is generated.
- Describe how heat flows through the atmosphere.
- Collect and interpret weather intelligence for your community.

Join the Team

Student Argonauts proudly stand in front of the Aerosonde that they helped Anthony Guillory construct at NASA Wallops Flight Facility. The Argonauts joined in preflight mission briefings, the launch and recovery of Aerosonde, and a post-flight debrief on the success of the mission. While at Wallops Flight Facility, the Argonauts also launched a weather balloon to collect more weather data. From left: Student Argonaut Ellen Drake, Teacher Argonaut Dawn Burbach, Host Researcher Anthony Guillory, and Student Argonauts Neil Muir and Cameron King.

Photo by Peter Haydock, The JASON Project

Trouble Brewing in Earth's Atmosphere

In September 2005, Hurricane Ophelia spun unpredictably off the coast of North Carolina but was beginning to weaken. Some computer models predicted that Ophelia would not make landfall. Other models predicted a direct hit on the East Coast. Ophelia's unusual behavior had the attention of the U. S. Air Force and the National Oceanic and Atmospheric Administration (NOAA). The storm presented a unique research opportunity for the National Aeronautics and Space Administration (NASA) as well. NASA planned to launch an uninhabited aerial vehicle (UAV) named Aerosonde into the storm. A small group of researchers stationed at NASA's Wallops Flight Facility in Virginia were patiently preparing to go into action with the little UAV.

The Air Force flew a WC-130J airplane into Ophelia at an altitude of 1500 m (4921 ft). NOAA sent in a larger WP-3D Orion aircraft at 3000 m (9842 ft). The intrepid Aerosonde's first hurricane mission would be at a mere 500 m (1640 ft)!

The Air Force and NOAA planes carried full crews to conduct their missions. Aerosonde carried only its payload of instruments. Onboard, a package of sophisticated instruments and software would measure wind speed, direction, altitude, position, sea surface temperature, air temperature, and humidity. The NASA flight support crew, coordinated by Anthony Guillory, NASA's flight manager at the Wallops Flight Facility, launched Aerosonde into Hurricane Ophelia, and successfully returned the craft to the base when its groundbreaking mission was completed. Aerosonde collected data more refined than the data collected by either of the other planes. The real prize in Aerosonde's data was a measurement of hurricane-strength winds at a time when Ophelia had been downgraded to a tropical storm.

With tools like Aerosonde, weather forecasters are able to predict the behavior of monster storms with increasing accuracy. Their predictions will help to save lives and protect property.

Your mission will also involve gathering critical weather intelligence. Work along with the Argonauts you will meet in this mission to learn how to anticipate the threat of a monster storm.

Mission 1 Briefing Video Prepare for your mission by viewing this briefing on your objectives. Learn about the atmospheric conditions that scientists measure to forecast monster storms.

Mission Briefing

Defining a Storm

Think about the most recent storm you have witnessed. What was it like? Was the wind howling? Was the rain falling so hard that it pounded the roof? Was lightning flashing all around?

Storms are weather events. Unlike less energetic changes in the air, storms are violent disturbances. Sometimes, they appear with little or no warning. When they strike, they are accompanied by strong winds, intense precipitation, and other extreme conditions.

Weather describes the state of the **atmosphere.** We often describe weather as measured values of wind speed, temperature, air pressure, precipitation, and humidity. Weather conditions at any location change over time. Typically, these changes are gradual and

predictable. However, when the change is sudden and energetic, beware! You are probably experiencing a storm.

Suppose that heavy rain and wind gusts powerful enough to knock over trash barrels should suddenly occur. No doubt you would consider that a storm. But suppose that the wind were powerful enough to knock down a building. Now, that is a monster storm!

There are all sorts of monster storms. **Hurricanes** are among the largest of these powerful disturbances. Hurricanes are highly organized storms that can generate ocean waves of about 30 m (98 ft) and deadly storm surges over 9 m (30 ft).

When atmospheric conditions are right, a **thunderstorm** can grow into a **supercell,** which can spawn a **tornado** or even several tornadoes. Although more compact in size than hurricanes, tornadoes pack a powerful and deadly punch. With wind speeds that

▲ Tornado touchdown near Alfalfa, Oklahoma.

can exceed 322 km/hr (200 mph), twisters can toss cars and flip mobile homes as if they were toys.

Lightning is an awesome electrical discharge that often accompanies hurricanes and tornadoes. A storm need not be a monster, however, to generate intense lightning. As long as weather conditions produce clouds having an unstable distribution of positive and negative charges, lightning can form.

Strong wind circulation may also produce a shower of irregular pieces of ice called **hail.** Although hail seldom grows larger than pea-sized, monster hailstones larger than baseballs have been recorded striking people and property!

When the temperature falls, the scene may be set for a different type of monster storm—a **blizzard.** A blizzard is a severe snowstorm with winds in excess of 56 km/h (35 mph) and visibilities of 0.4 km (0.25 mi) or less for an extended period of time. Unlike those of a typical winter storm, the blizzard's strong winds and heavy snow produce blinding conditions. In a blizzard's most extreme form, snow-laden winds create a complete whiteout. During such an intense period, so much snow fills the air that an observer cannot tell the sky from the ground.

Not all extreme weather arrives as a sudden or an intense disturbance, however. Extreme weather can develop slowly and gradually. Although such

Fast Fact

Ten percent of all thunderstorms produce either hail, wind gusts over 93 km/h (58 mph), or a tornado. When a thunderstorm produces any one or more of these events, meteorologists classify it as a severe thunderstorm.

▲ Hailstones the size of baseballs have occasionally accompanied tornadic storms.

incremental change may lack the forceful onset of a tornado or hurricane, the effects of gradual change can have long-lasting consequences.

Have you ever experienced a **drought?** If so, you know that a drought is a prolonged period of below-normal rainfall. Over time, a drought will produce severe effects that range from crop loss to frequent wildfires. Droughts can cause a community to change the ways it uses and conserves water. In a state of emergency, communities will enforce laws that strictly regulate the use of the endangered water supply.

Now imagine a period of greater-than-normal rainfall. Over-abundant rainfall, even when it is not part of the drenching from a monster storm, can produce dangerous **floods.** As the ground becomes inundated, it can no longer absorb water. This **runoff** then collects in low-lying areas. In cities, streets and highways may become flooded and impassable. In rural regions, if enough precipitation accumulates, streams and rivers will spill over their banks and submerge surrounding areas.

Prolonged periods of excessively hot or cold weather can also be extreme. A **heat wave** is a period of above-average temperatures. During summer months, heat waves can be deadly to humans, pets, livestock, and crops. Demands for air conditioning may strain electrical power grids and result in blackouts or partial power outages called brownouts.

Drops in temperature can be just as deadly. During winter months, extended periods of below-freezing temperatures produce life-threatening situations. Heating systems fail. Cars refuse to start. Water pipes freeze and burst. These circumstances only add to the dangers of extreme cold.

Forecasters collect measurements on atmospheric conditions, then predict each day's weather. Each measurement provides a clue to what the weather is doing and how it might change within a few hours. Experienced forecasters can be very accurate in predicting the weather several days out from the data collected.

Researchers use many tools and instruments to piece together the big picture. With more research and better instruments, scientists hope to increase the accuracy of weather forecasts. When lives and property are on the line, accurate forecasting is critical.

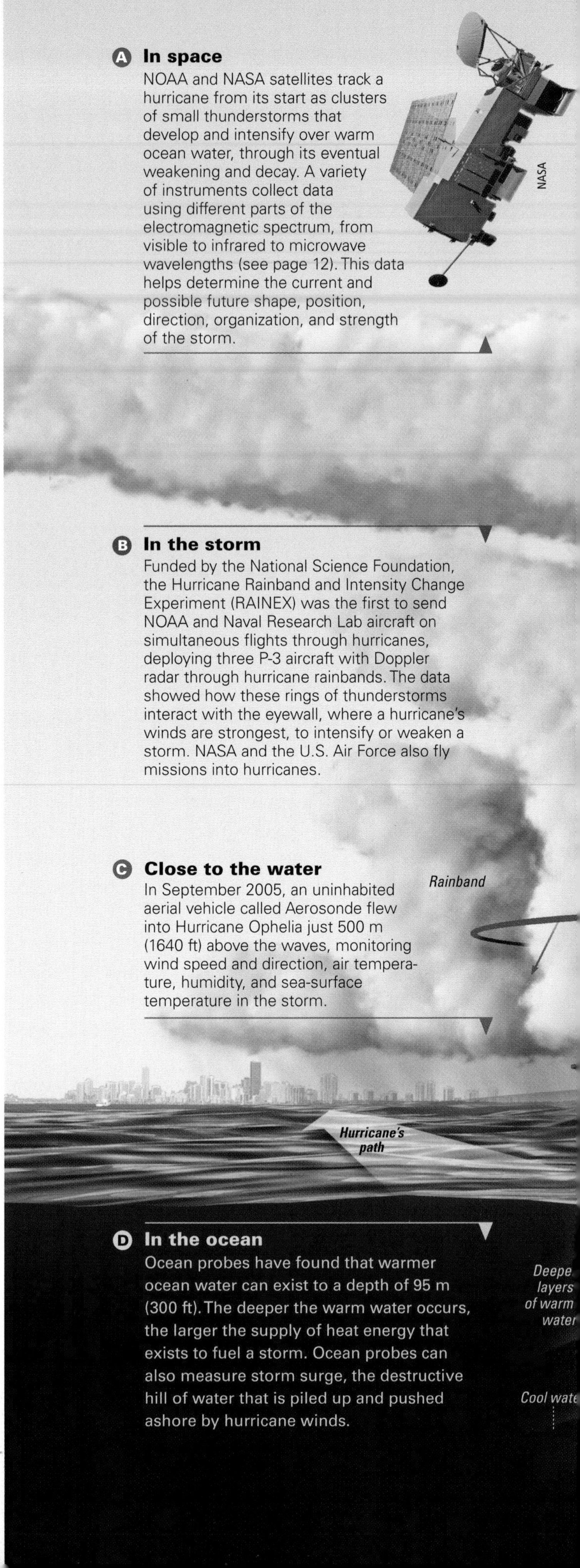

► This illustration shows a striking composite of many of the aerial vehicles and other instruments that scientists use to collect tropical storm and hurricane data over and under the ocean.

Ⓐ In space
NOAA and NASA satellites track a hurricane from its start as clusters of small thunderstorms that develop and intensify over warm ocean water, through its eventual weakening and decay. A variety of instruments collect data using different parts of the electromagnetic spectrum, from visible to infrared to microwave wavelengths (see page 12). This data helps determine the current and possible future shape, position, direction, organization, and strength of the storm.

Ⓑ In the storm
Funded by the National Science Foundation, the Hurricane Rainband and Intensity Change Experiment (RAINEX) was the first to send NOAA and Naval Research Lab aircraft on simultaneous flights through hurricanes, deploying three P-3 aircraft with Doppler radar through hurricane rainbands. The data showed how these rings of thunderstorms interact with the eyewall, where a hurricane's winds are strongest, to intensify or weaken a storm. NASA and the U.S. Air Force also fly missions into hurricanes.

Ⓒ Close to the water
In September 2005, an uninhabited aerial vehicle called Aerosonde flew into Hurricane Ophelia just 500 m (1640 ft) above the waves, monitoring wind speed and direction, air temperature, humidity, and sea-surface temperature in the storm.

Rainband

Hurricane's path

Ⓓ In the ocean
Ocean probes have found that warmer ocean water can exist to a depth of 95 m (300 ft). The deeper the warm water occurs, the larger the supply of heat energy that exists to fuel a storm. Ocean probes can also measure storm surge, the destructive hill of water that is piled up and pushed ashore by hurricane winds.

Deeper layers of warm water

Cool water

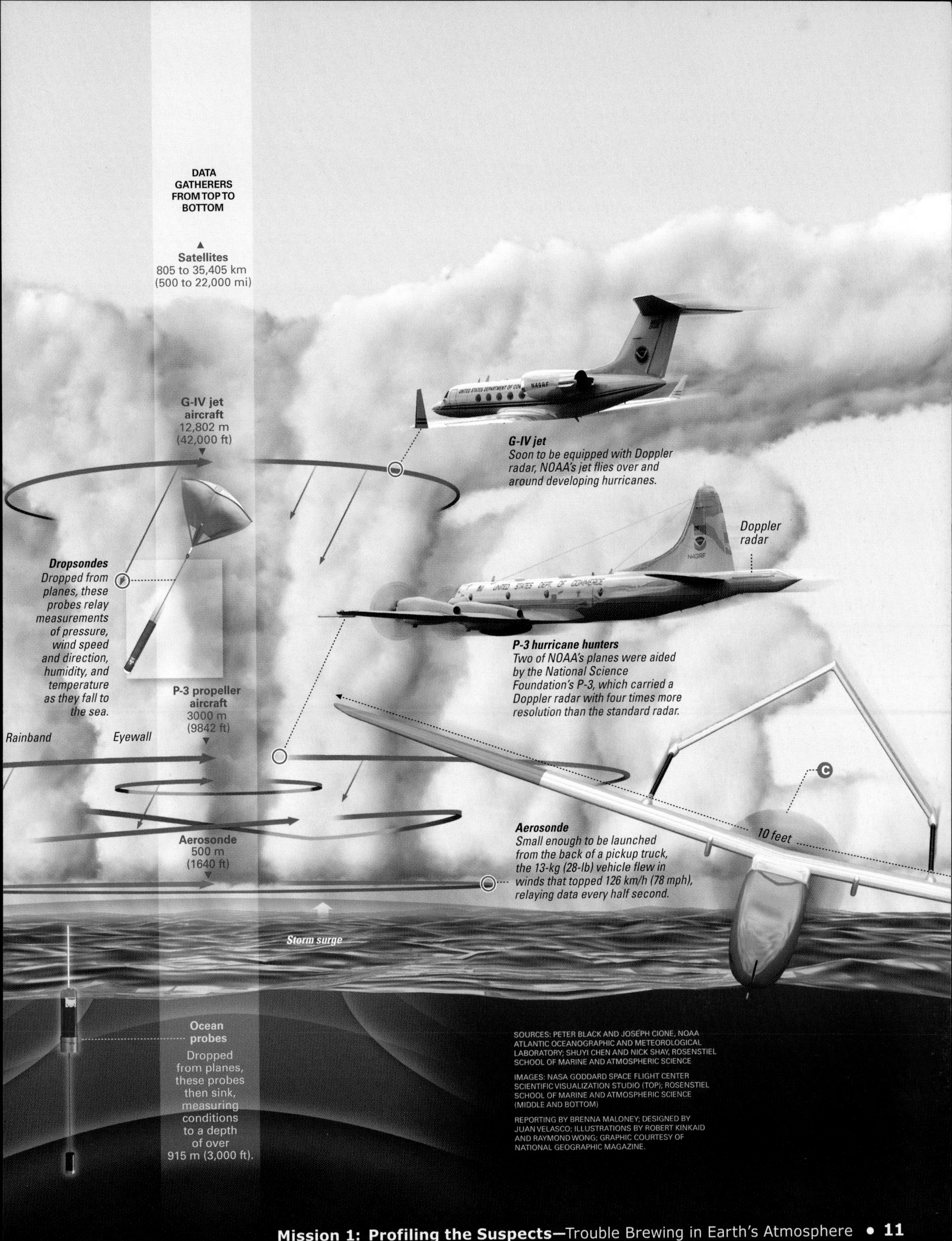

DATA GATHERERS FROM TOP TO BOTTOM

▲ **Satellites**
805 to 35,405 km
(500 to 22,000 mi)

G-IV jet aircraft
12,802 m
(42,000 ft)

G-IV jet
Soon to be equipped with Doppler radar, NOAA's jet flies over and around developing hurricanes.

Dropsondes
Dropped from planes, these probes relay measurements of pressure, wind speed and direction, humidity, and temperature as they fall to the sea.

Doppler radar

P-3 hurricane hunters
Two of NOAA's planes were aided by the National Science Foundation's P-3, which carried a Doppler radar with four times more resolution than the standard radar.

P-3 propeller aircraft
3000 m
(9842 ft)

Rainband   Eyewall

C

10 feet

Aerosonde
500 m
(1640 ft)

Aerosonde
Small enough to be launched from the back of a pickup truck, the 13-kg (28-lb) vehicle flew in winds that topped 126 km/h (78 mph), relaying data every half second.

Storm surge

Ocean probes
Dropped from planes, these probes then sink, measuring conditions to a depth of over 915 m (3,000 ft).

SOURCES: PETER BLACK AND JOSEPH CIONE, NOAA ATLANTIC OCEANOGRAPHIC AND METEOROLOGICAL LABORATORY; SHUYI CHEN AND NICK SHAY, ROSENSTIEL SCHOOL OF MARINE AND ATMOSPHERIC SCIENCE

IMAGES: NASA GODDARD SPACE FLIGHT CENTER SCIENTIFIC VISUALIZATION STUDIO (TOP); ROSENSTIEL SCHOOL OF MARINE AND ATMOSPHERIC SCIENCE (MIDDLE AND BOTTOM)

REPORTING BY BRENNA MALONEY; DESIGNED BY JUAN VELASCO; ILLUSTRATIONS BY ROBERT KINKAID AND RAYMOND WONG; GRAPHIC COURTESY OF NATIONAL GEOGRAPHIC MAGAZINE.

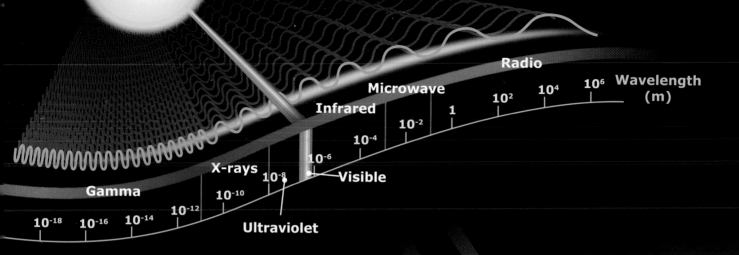

Gamma | X-rays | Ultraviolet | Visible | Infrared | Microwave | Radio

Wavelength (m): 10^{-18} 10^{-16} 10^{-14} 10^{-12} 10^{-10} 10^{-8} 10^{-6} 10^{-4} 10^{-2} 1 10^{2} 10^{4} 10^{6}

Energy from the Sun

Where does a monster storm's energy come from? Would you believe its energy could be traced to a place 150 million kilometers (93 million miles) away? In fact, most of the energy that drives Earth's weather and climate comes from this place. Perhaps you have heard of it. It is called the sun.

Within the sun, nuclear reactions produce an immense amount of energy that streams outward into space as electromagnetic radiation.

The sun produces the full range of electromagnetic radiation in what is known as the electromagnetic spectrum. Most of the sun's radiation travels outward as three types of waves: infrared (IR) radiation, visible light, and ultraviolet (UV) radiation. These waves travel through space at the same speed but are distinguished from one another by their wavelength. Of the three types of waves, infrared and visible light waves make up the majority of the radiation that reaches Earth.

Although your eyes cannot detect IR radiation, you can feel it. That is because your skin absorbs infrared radiation and heats up.

The visible portion of the sun's electromagnetic spectrum contains the colors of light that your eyes can detect.

The third type of radiation, ultraviolet (UV) radiation, like infrared radiation, cannot be detected by your eyes. UV radiation can have harmful effects on living tissue. Fortunately, the ozone layer in Earth's atmosphere filters out most of this harmful radiation before it reaches the ground.

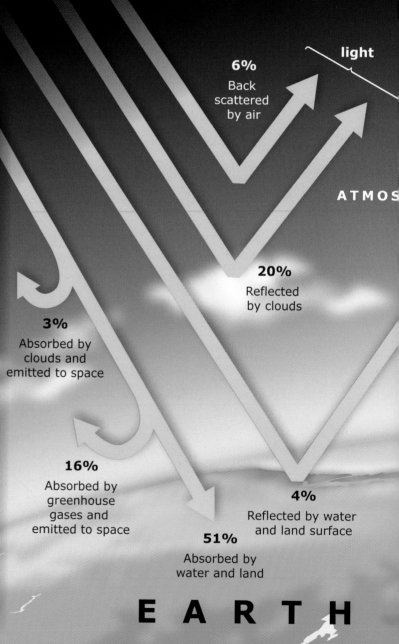

light

6% Back scattered by air

20% Reflected by clouds

3% Absorbed by clouds and emitted to space

16% Absorbed by greenhouse gases and emitted to space

51% Absorbed by water and land

4% Reflected by water and land surface

ATMOS

EARTH

Striking the Earth

Clouds, air molecules, and particles (aerosols) reflect or absorb about half of the sunlight that reaches Earth's atmosphere. The rest of the sunlight strikes the surface below.

As light strikes Earth's surface, things begin to heat up. Air just above the warmed surface absorbs some of the released infrared radiation. This transfer of heat from Earth's surface to air energizes the atmosphere and produces our planet's weather.

This process is not uniformly spread around the globe. Landforms, bodies of water, vegetation, buildings, and roads influence the amount and the rate of heat absorption and transfer.

The Greenhouse Effect

Like other resources, heat can be recycled. This natural reuse and retention of atmospheric heat is called the greenhouse effect. Certain heat-retaining

gases—called greenhouse gases—such as water vapor, carbon dioxide, methane and ozone are the primary molecules that retain this heat in the air.

Here is how the basic process works. Solar energy that strikes our planet's surface warms the ground. As the ground cools, heat is released to the atmosphere through conduction and convection. This is called sensible heat. Greenhouse gases readily absorb this energy, preventing its immediate release back into space. Also, when liquid water on Earth absorbs energy and changes state to water vapor, energy called latent heat energy is carried into the atmosphere. As you would expect, all of this retained heat warms the atmosphere.

In a balanced state, the amount of solar energy striking our planet will equal the amount released back into space. Thus with a stable greenhouse effect, our global temperature should remain elevated, but steady. In fact, some scientists report that the greenhouse effect has produced an environment about 35°C (63°F) warmer than it would be if there were no heat recycling.

These days, however, there seems to be less heat leaving the global system. This has produced a slow-but-steady rise in the average temperature of the oceans and atmosphere. This trend is called global warming. Global warming events have occurred many times in the geological history of our planet.

Many scientists have concluded that human activities, including the burning of fossil fuels, have contributed to this current increase in the levels of greenhouse gases. This has produced an atmosphere that retains increasing amounts of heat energy. The extra load of thermal energy not only warms the atmosphere, but increases Earth's surface temperatures. More heat retention also results in a gradual rise in sea temperature.

The increased heat content of warmer seas and atmosphere may alter critical balances. Increased temperatures can melt ice, resulting in a rise in sea level. The higher temperatures may negatively impact Earth's ecosystems. In addition, as sea temperatures rise, more energy is available to fuel monster storm systems.

Scientists are closely monitoring retreating glaciers, increasing sea-surface temperatures, and the frequency of monster storms. These things may indicate that the climate of Earth is changing.

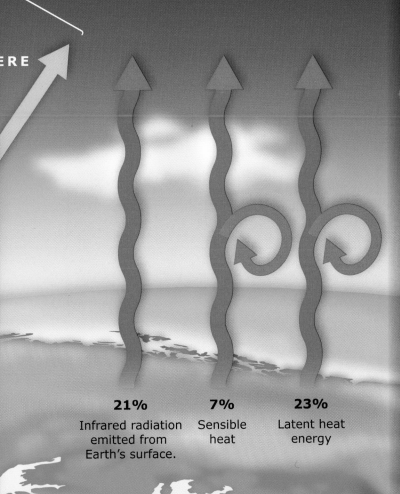

ERE

21%
Infrared radiation emitted from Earth's surface.

7%
Sensible heat

23%
Latent heat energy

Air and Air Pressure

Take a deep breath. As you inhale, your lungs fill with a mixture of molecules and a small number of single atoms.

Air is composed of many different molecules and atoms in a gaseous state. On average, nitrogen molecules make up about 78 percent of the gases in air. Oxygen molecules account for another 21 percent of air. Carbon dioxide, argon, and other rare gases make up the remaining one percent. The amount of water vapor in the atmosphere varies. Depending on the weather, water vapor can make up from zero to four percent of the gases in air.

Although you cannot see it, you live at the bottom of an ocean of air. Every molecule and atom of air is pulled down by gravity. At Earth's surface, the accumulated weight of all of this air produces a pressure of one atmosphere. Meteorologists, however, usually use other units to measure air pressure. Scientists more often use the unit millibar (mb) or the unit hectopascal (hPa) to measure **air pressure.** We experience a standard air pressure of 1013.25 mb = 1 atmosphere at sea level. Converting this value to hectopascals is easy. One millibar is equal to one hectopascal, so Earth's standard air pressure in hectopascals is 1013.25 hPa.

Unlike solids and liquids, gases are easily compressed. The weight of the air above compresses, or squeezes together, air closer to the Earth's surface. Because more molecules and atoms are in a smaller space, collisions occur more frequently. Every time a molecule or an atom of air strikes something, it exerts a force. When atoms and molecules are squeezed closer together, more collisions occur and the force is greater. The greater force produces a higher air pressure, which is the force exerted on an area or surface in contact with the air.

When air pressure changes, the weather usually changes. An increase in air pressure typically indicates clear skies, more sun, less wind, and drier weather ahead. If the air pressure begins to decrease, just the opposite is probably ahead—clouds, less sun, more wind, and possibly precipitation of some kind.

Anthony Guillory's team uses Aerosonde to collect air pressure data in the atmosphere. These measurements recorded along the flight path can help researchers understand a storm and predict its behavior. Is the storm intensifying? Is it weakening? The low air pressure measurements collected by Aerosonde typically occur in strong tropical storms and hurricanes.

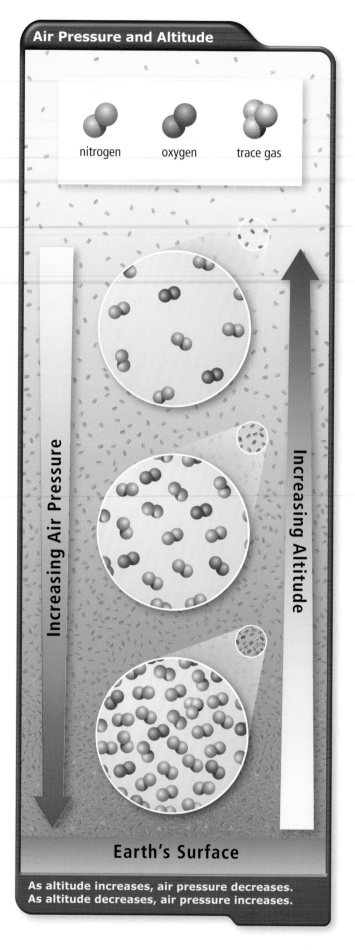

Air Pressure and Altitude

nitrogen oxygen trace gas

Increasing Air Pressure

Increasing Altitude

Earth's Surface

As altitude increases, air pressure decreases.
As altitude decreases, air pressure increases.

Team Highlight

CAMERON KING
Student Argonaut, Ohio

Cameron King helps Dave Smith mount Aerosonde on top of a truck so that the Argonauts can launch the aircraft. Aerosonde measures air temperature, wind speed, wind direction, sea-surface temperature, and barometric pressure within a hurricane.

Photo by Peter Haydock, The JASON Project

NEIL MUIR
Student Argonaut, New York

Argonaut Neil Muir tries his hand at navigating the remotely controlled Aerosonde. After Aerosonde is launched, a navigator guides the UAV out of the airspace. An onboard computer with global positioning system (GPS) capability then takes over and flies the aircraft into and back from the storm.

Photo by Peter Haydock, The JASON Project

Wind

As you rise in the atmosphere, air pressure decreases because fewer and fewer air molecules are above you. However, you do not have to change altitude to encounter a change in air pressure. The concentration of gas particles, and therefore the air pressure, can differ in neighboring air masses. Air will move from a region with higher pressure to a region with lower pressure. This movement produces **wind.**

How are high and low air pressure regions created? Air pressure differences result from the uneven heating of Earth and the atmosphere. As air gains heat energy, its molecules and atoms move faster and spread out. This produces an air mass having low pressure. If an air mass cools, its particles slow down and become more concentrated, producing an air mass with high pressure. The pressure difference between different air masses causes wind to blow from regions of higher pressure to regions of lower pressure. The wind's speed depends on the pressure difference, and is influenced as well by Earth's rotation. The greater the pressure difference is, the faster the wind blows.

Using Aerosonde, NASA and NOAA can measure hurricane strength wind speeds without putting a flight crew and research scientists in danger. Having the capability of flying lower than any piloted aircraft, Aerosonde can collect data at altitudes that are much closer to where we live. These measurements provide better information about how the storm is behaving.

Aerosonde

A remotely piloted, uninhabited aerial vehicle (UAV) that monitors, records, and transmits weather data. Its rapid and internally-generated corrections to its flight path allow the craft to maneuver within hurricane force winds.

Data Probe Specifications:

Range: 3000 km (1864 mi)

Payload: 5 kg (11 lb) that can include weather sensor pods for air pressure, temperature, and humidity

Wingspan: 2.9 m (9.5 ft)

Mass: 13–15 kg (29–33 lb)

Thrust: Propeller driven by a 24cc gasoline engine (similar to a model airplane engine)

Composition: Fiberglass tail, fiberglass and graphite wing, graphite tube tailbooms, carbon fiber fuselage, and Kevlar nose cone

Fuel tank: 5 kg (11 lb) of premium unleaded gasoline

Aerosonde was the first remotely piloted aircraft to cross the Atlantic Ocean (3270 km; 2032 mi), a journey it completed in 26 hours and 45 minutes.

Unlike a typical airplane, Aerosonde does not have a separate vertical stabilizer (fin) and horizontal stabilizer in the tail section. Instead, it has an inverted "v" shaped tail that maintains craft stability.

The nose cone of Aerosonde is made of Kevlar, the same lightweight and strong fiber material used to make body armor.

Measuring Weather: Air Pressure, Precipitation, and Temperature

Scientists like Anthony Guillory use weather measurements such as wind speed, wind direction, air pressure, air temperature, and precipitation amounts to help them understand the weather. Data must be collected at many locations in order for forecasters to predict future weather events. Placing measurement tools at various locations on the ground and in the air at different altitudes can help make weather forecasts more accurate. The important thing for scientists is gathering enough information at the right locations and then making a prediction based on their experience and the data they have gathered. This is not as easy as it might sound.

In the case of a hurricane, each measurement indicates something different about the behavior of the storm. As each measurement is considered, patterns may begin to reveal the future of the storm. For instance, the lower the air pressure at the center of the hurricane, the stronger the storm is at that time. As air pressure in the hurricane begins to rise, scientists may predict that the storm is beginning to weaken. Forecasters can use this information to make predictions about a hurricane's formation, growth, and decay that are useful for emergency planning.

How else can air pressure figure into a typical weather forecast? When air pressure is higher at one location than at another, the air will move from the higher pressure zone to the lower pressure zone. This movement of air creates wind. We can use a tool called a barometer to measure the rise and fall of air pressure at a given location. Measuring air pressure can help us predict the weather in the near future. What do the other measurements tell us about the current and future weather?

In this lab, you will build and use a several weather measurement tools to do your own weather study.

Materials
- **Lab 1 Data Sheet**
- **barometer tool** (p. 112)
- **wind vane tool** (p. 112)
- **anemometer tool** (p. 113)
- **rain gauge** (p. 113)
- **thermometer**
- **compass**

Lab Prep
Build, calibrate, and practice using your barometer, rain gauge, anemometer, and wind vane. Familiarize yourself with using your thermometer and compass. Then, answer the following questions.

1. How does your barometer tool work? Include as much detail as possible.

2. What are the measurement limitations of your barometer? How accurate is your barometer? How can you test the accuracy of your barometer?

3. If the barometer needle drops, how would you expect the weather to change? Why?

4. If the barometer needle rises, how would you expect the weather to change? Why?

5. Could barometer data alone be used to predict the weather? Why or why not?

6. Research other types of barometers. How are they similar to and different from the one you built?

7. Could your wind vane be used to forecast the weather? Could the anemometer or thermometer be used without the other tools to forecast the weather? Explain why each tool can or cannot be used to forecast weather on its own.

8. Why do you need all of the tools to establish the current and future weather?

9. What are the limitations of each of your tools for data gathering?

10. Discuss the difference between accuracy (correctness of your findings) and precision (repeatability of your findings) when collecting data. How accurate and precise are the tools you built? Explain.

11. If you had access to weather data collection tools that you knew to be accurate, how do you think your data would compare to data collected by those tools? Could you use those tools to calibrate your tools? Why or why not? Would it improve the accuracy of the data you collect? Explain.

Make Observations

1. Use your tools to measure atmospheric pressure, wind speed and direction, temperature, and rainfall for a period of at least one week. Why is it important to collect data for more than one day?

2. What can you tell about the weather during this time period? Is it changing? How?

3. Construct graphs for the following data sets: temperature, wind speed, rainfall, and barometric pressure. Plot each set of data versus time. Indicate wind direction for each data point on your wind speed graph. Do you see any trends among these graphs?

4. Can you use your measurements to make any inferences or predictions about the weather?

5. Use the National Weather Service Web site (*http://www.nws.noaa.gov/*) to compare your observations with official recorded data. Go to the Web site and enter your zip code in the "Local Forecast" box.

6. How different were your measurements from those you found online? Why are they different?

7. Your barometer tool cannot measure pressure in millibars. How can you compare your air pressure measurements to those you found online?

8. Now that you have gathered these measurements, make some weather predictions for the next seven days. What measurements will be most helpful in making predictions?

9. Compare your predictions with the weather that actually occurs. What measurements proved to be the most informative about upcoming weather? What conclusions can you draw about your measurements and the weather you observed?

10. Would using data from the Internet allow you to make better predictions for your location? Why or why not?

11. Do you see any relationships among the measurements taken? Explain what you observed and why you think relationships do or do not exist.

 Journal Question As you read in the Mission Briefing, air pressure decreases as you move higher in the atmosphere. How do you think air pressure affects athletes who compete at higher elevations? How do you think air pressure affects athletes who compete at sea level?

▲ Extreme weather events can have devastating effects on people and their property.

Fast Fact

Mountain climbers must contend with a very serious problem—continually decreasing air density as they climb higher. On Mount Everest, the world's highest peak (8850 m, or 29,035 ft), air pressure is about 300 mb, less than one-third of standard sea-level air pressure. Here, you must breathe three times as much air to get the same amount of oxygen that you would get at sea level! The ratio of particles is the same, but the density is different.

Pushing Up with Pressure

When Aerosonde was launched, air pressure measurements were collected and entered into a computer program able to use this data to determine the wind speeds and wind directions in Hurricane Ophelia. In the future, forecasters will be able to use Aerosonde data to better predict where winds would be strongest in a hurricane. Then, forecasters and emergency management personnel will be better prepared when a hurricane makes landfall.

In this lab, you will investigate the strength of air pressure.

Materials
- Lab 2 Data Sheet
- small paper or plastic drinking cup
- small basin (such as a bowl)
- index card (or playing card)
- pushpin
- piece of tape

Lab Prep

1. As you learned in the Mission Briefing, air pressure is caused by moving molecules and atoms. Do you think that air pressure acts in all directions? Why or why not?

2. If the air pressure outside a container is higher than the air pressure inside the container, an overall inward push exists on the container. What would happen if a hole were made in the container?

3. Do you think it is possible to keep water in an upside-down cup using only a piece of paper? Why or why not?

Make Observations

1. Fill a small drinking cup to the top rim with water and place the index card on top of the cup. Hold the cup over a basin or sink. CAREFULLY turn the cup upside down while holding the card firmly in place. Then release your hand from the card while still holding the cup. What happens?

2. Why does the water behave as it does?

3. Try the activity again, but first use a push-pin to poke a small hole in the bottom of the cup. Cover the hole with tape, and then repeat step one. While the cup is upside down, remove the tape from the bottom of the cup. What happens?

4. Why is the behavior of the water different when the tape is removed from the cup?

5. What do you think would happen if you put the hole in the side of the cup instead of the bottom?

6. Does the size of the cup matter? Why or why not?

7. How much air can you let into the cup while it is upside down and still keep the water in the cup?

8. If you use a liquid other than water, will the activity still work? Try it! What happens?

 Journal Question Using your knowledge of air pressure, explain what happens as you drink through a straw.

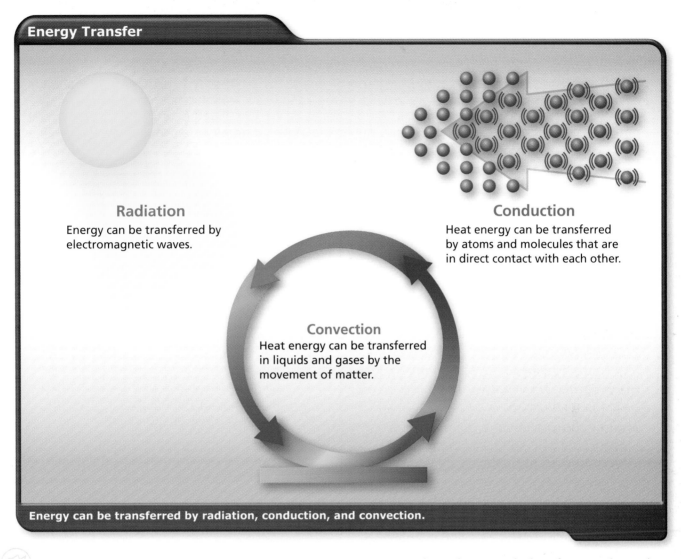

Radiation
Energy can be transferred by electromagnetic waves.

Conduction
Heat energy can be transferred by atoms and molecules that are in direct contact with each other.

Convection
Heat energy can be transferred in liquids and gases by the movement of matter.

Energy can be transferred by radiation, conduction, and convection.

Heat Flow in Our Atmosphere

Heat energy does not stay in the same place. It flows from hotter places to cooler places. If enough time is allowed to pass, the two places will reach the same temperature and heat will stop flowing. There are three different ways by which heat energy can be transferred.

Radiation—Energy transferred by electromagnetic radiation. The flow of energy from the sun to Earth is an example of radiation.

Conduction—Heat energy can also be transferred between atoms and molecules that are in direct contact. If you have ever touched a hot frying pan, you experienced heat transfer by conduction. Heat flowed from the hot pan to your hand.

Convection—In materials that are capable of flow, such as liquids and gases, heat energy can be transferred by the movement of matter. Warmer liquids and gases are less dense and therefore tend to rise, displacing cooler material, which is forced to sink. This movement forms a convection. This process is very important in transferring heat energy in thunderstorms and hurricanes.

Team Highlight

Argonauts Ellen Drake, Neil Muir, Dawn Burbach, and Cameron King help Ryan Vu assemble Aerosonde.

Observing Convection

When studying a monster storm, scientists like Anthony Guillory measure temperature data from the air and from the water bodies that their planes and UAVs fly over. This information is important because it helps scientists predict how strong the winds might become.

Convection is a process that helps distribute heat energy from Earth's surface into the atmosphere. Under the right conditions, this process fuels monster storms. Convection also occurs beneath Earth's surface in the mantle, where currents of slowly flowing molten rock help move the massive tectonic plates that make up Earth's outer layer. Convection in the oceans also helps mix water layers and distributes heat. In this lab, you will observe this process on a very small scale using just soap and water!

Materials
- Lab 3 Data Sheet
- pearlized soap
- beaker or glass
- tablespoon
- bowl
- ice cubes
- warm water
- room-temperature water
- flashlight (optional)

Lab Prep

1. Fill the beaker with room-temperature water and add about a tablespoon of pearlized liquid soap. Mix the soap into the water. What happens?

2. Place the beaker in the bowl and fill the bowl with warm water. Place some ice cubes in the beaker. What does the mixture do?

3. Describe the heat transfer occurring in this experiment.

4. What do you think would happen to the movement of the soap if you let the beaker sit for an hour?

5. How does this activity model the movement of air in the atmosphere (or the movement of water in the oceans)?

Make Observations

1. Design and implement an experiment to answer one of the following questions. Have your teacher approve your design before you start.

a. Does the size or shape of the container (the beaker or glass in the Lab Prep) affect the way convection currents move?

b. What happens if objects that get in the way of the soap's movement are placed at the bottom of the container?

c. Does a larger temperature difference between the inside and the outside of the container have a major effect on the movement of the soap?

2. How does your experiment help answer the research question that you chose?

 Journal Question Earth receives more heat at the equator than at the poles. How do wind currents result? What is the overall effect of winds on Earth?

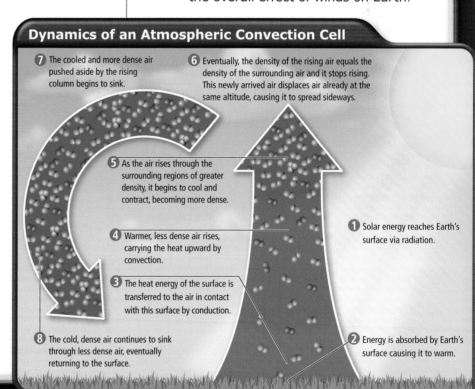

Dynamics of an Atmospheric Convection Cell

7. The cooled and more dense air pushed aside by the rising column begins to sink.

6. Eventually, the density of the rising air equals the density of the surrounding air and it stops rising. This newly arrived air displaces air already at the same altitude, causing it to spread sideways.

5. As the air rises through the surrounding regions of greater density, it begins to cool and contract, becoming more dense.

4. Warmer, less dense air rises, carrying the heat upward by convection.

3. The heat energy of the surface is transferred to the air in contact with this surface by conduction.

1. Solar energy reaches Earth's surface via radiation.

8. The cold, dense air continues to sink through less dense air, eventually returning to the surface.

2. Energy is absorbed by Earth's surface causing it to warm.

Profile of a Storm

Photo by Peter Haydock, The JASON Project

Recall that your mission is to *gather critical weather intelligence for your community so that you can anticipate the threat of a monster storm.* Now that you have been fully briefed, it is time to collect and interpret weather intelligence.

In September 2005, Anthony Guillory helped NASA collect data about Hurricane Ophelia that could not have been captured without Aerosonde. Flying at 500 m (1640 ft), Aerosonde measured wind speeds different from those measured by the WP-3D plane flying through the storm at 3000 m (9842 ft). Because we live far below the high altitudes at which the NOAA plane flies (and even below the height at which Aerosonde flies), scientists at NASA and NOAA are researching such storms at lower altitudes to see whether they can make better storm forecasts from this new data set. In this activity, you will use wind speeds recorded by Aerosonde and the WP-3D research plane to determine how wind speeds differ at various altitudes in a hurricane.

After you have analyzed NASA's data, you will apply your new knowledge and skills in and around your school. First, you will build a wind profile in the classroom and collect data on other weather conditions that might influence wind. Then you will design a weather observation protocol that will help you determine the best locations around your school to take weather measurements and anticipate the threat of a monster storm.

Objectives: To complete your mission, accomplish the following objectives:

- Compare NASA's Aerosonde data to NOAA's WP-3D data.

- Design and document a procedure to collect weather intelligence about wind fields in your classroom and outside of your school.

- Enter your weather intelligence in a data collection chart online or on paper.

Mission 1 Argonaut Field Assignment Video Join the National Argonauts as they launch an Aerosonde flight at Wallops Island, Virginia.

Aerosonde and WP-3D Flights

WP-3D NOAA

3000 m

2500 m

2000 m

1500 m

1000 m

Aerosonde NASA

500 m

Ocean Surface

Hurricane Ophelia Wind Map

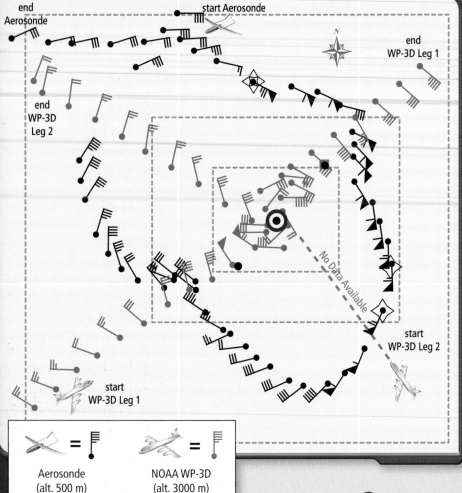

Aerosonde (alt. 500 m) = [wind barb symbol]

NOAA WP-3D (alt. 3000 m) = [wind barb symbol]

Materials

- **Mission 1 Field Assignment Data Sheets**
- **Wind Barb Activity Master**
- **barometer tool** (p. 112)
- **wind vane tool** (p. 112)
- **anemometer tool** (p. 113)
- **rain gauge** (p. 113)
- **thermometer**
- **3-speed fans (4)**
- **masking tape**
- **red, black, and green markers**
- **magnetic compass**

Caution! Exercise caution when using electrical devices in lab experiments. Be sure to keep hands and objects clear of fans when they are in operation.

Field Preparation

Look at the Hurricane Ophelia wind map on the left. Use the chart on the inside back cover of this book to learn how to read wind barbs like those shown in the diagram. Compare the measurements taken by Aerosonde with those taken by the WP-3D. Note that hurricane-force winds measure 64 knots (119 km/h, 74 mph) or greater. In the Ophelia wind map, hurricane force winds have been identified with a diamond shape around the **wind barb.**

1. Download the Wind Barb Activity from the JASON Mission Center and complete the exercises in the activity. This will help you read the wind field map above.

2. Describe, compare, and contrast the flight paths of NOAA's WP-3D and NASA's Aerosonde.

3. Why do you think these aircraft flew different flight patterns and altitudes?

4. According to the data collected by Aerosonde, in which direction does the storm rotate, clockwise or counter-clockwise?

5. Does the data collected by the WP-3D support your answer to question 4? Explain.

6. Which aircraft recorded the highest wind speed? What were the highest three measurements? At what altitude were these measurements taken?

7. In which part of the storm do you see the closest and most dramatic changes in wind direction? What is this portion of a hurricane called?

Now build a model of NASA's research.

8 Your teacher will position several floor fans around the perimeter of a grid that models the winds patterns of Hurricane Ophelia and maps the flights of Aerosonde and the WP-3D. Use the anemometer and wind vane tools to measure the wind speed and direction at one meter from the ground along the alpha flight pattern of the WP-3D plane. Place masking tape on the grid and mark it with a red marker to identify each point along the flight path where you will take a data reading. How many data points do you need? Make a table to display your data.

9 Use the flight pattern of Aerosonde to perform the same wind speed and direction measurements about 17 cm (7 in.) from the ground. Use the black marker on the masking tape to identify each point along the flight path where you will take a data reading. Record this data in your table as well.

   a. Do you see differences in the measurements from the two altitudes and paths?

   b. Where do you see differences, if any?

   c. Why do you think the wind speed or direction is different at those places?

10 Taken all together, what does the data you collected tell you about the storm?

Mission Challenge

Your mission challenge is to design a process that will determine the best location around your school or home to collect wind, temperature, rainfall, and air pressure data. Answer the following questions before you go into the field.

1 Where do you think the best location around your school or home would be for a weather data collection site? Why?

2 What differences would you expect to see in the measurements at other potential locations around your school or home? Why?

3 Does the height at which you take the measurements make a difference? Explain.

4 How many data locations do you think you need to sample to confirm the selection of a single, good location for your weather station? How many times will you collect data at each possible location? Explain.

5 Does the time of day, month, or year matter for your data collection? Why or why not?

Carry out the procedure you designed in order to determine your final weather data collection location.

Mission Debrief

1 Make wind, temperature, rainfall, and air pressure maps for each location.

2 Choose a final location for your weather station. Explain why you think this is the best location. How does the data support your choice?

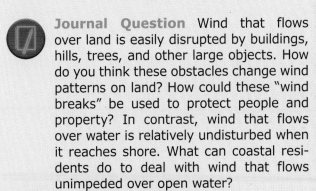

Journal Question Wind that flows over land is easily disrupted by buildings, hills, trees, and other large objects. How do you think these obstacles change wind patterns on land? How could these "wind breaks" be used to protect people and property? In contrast, wind that flows over water is relatively undisturbed when it reaches shore. What can coastal residents do to deal with wind that flows unimpeded over open water?

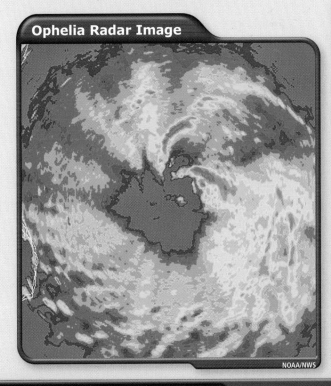

Ophelia Radar Image

NOAA/NWS

SUNKEN TREASURE, PIRATES & MONSTER STORMS

It was hurricane season in the year 1715. The treasure fleet had been waiting to return to Spain for nearly two years. Finally, the order was given to sail. So on a calm July day, eleven ships left Cuba. They sailed north to enter the Gulf Stream and travel within its moving waters across the Atlantic Ocean.

The riches carried by this fleet included silver and gold taken from the mines of the New World. Indians, the original inhabitants of these lands, were used as forced labor to remove these riches. When the Indians began dying in great numbers from disease and ill treatment, the Spaniards brought enslaved people from Africa.

Now, however, the treasure was needed in Spain. It was time to weigh anchor and transport this wealth to Europe. By itself, a ship full of treasure was an appealing prize for pirates. That is why these vessels did not sail alone. They traveled in fleets, protected by the combined firepower of several ships.

As these eleven vessels traveled north, they enjoyed fair weather. For five days, the fleet remained on course, pushed by a steady breeze and the waters of the Gulf Stream current. In these conditions, it was easy to steer clear of the jagged reefs that fringed the Florida coast. But things were about to change. A monster storm was fast approaching.

On July 30, the sailors awoke to increasing winds from the east. The blustery weather and the ocean swells were clues that a tropical storm was on its way. The captains gave orders to point the ships into the wind. It was a tactic used to prevent the storm from blowing the ships westward, onto the deadly offshore reefs.

For hours, the sailors battled against the ever increasing winds. At 4 A.M., the hurricane raged in all of its fury. The ships could no longer hold their own. The storm's winds and waves drove the ships westward toward the shallow coastline. There, one by one, the vessels struck offshore reefs and were torn apart. All eleven ships were lost and over 1000 sailors perished.

Many survivors did make it to shore. There, they outfitted a small boat. A group of survivors hoped to sail the boat back to Cuba to alert their comrades of the sinking. The

mission was a success! Within two weeks, help arrived and the stranded sailors were rescued.

Along with the rescuers came salvage crews. Looking for the treasure, these men dived and explored the wreck sites. From boats, they dragged the shallow bottom with large hooks. Their efforts paid off. Within a few months, the salvage teams had recovered over five million pieces of eight!

Good news traveled fast—and so did pirates. The salvage camp had treasure, but very few defenders. The pirate captain Henry Jennings decided it was time to redistribute the riches that the Spaniards had taken. Jennings and his men attacked the salvage camp. Without any loss of life, they overpowered sixty soldiers. To the pirate victors went over 120,000 pieces of eight, two cannons and several guns. For Jennings, things got even better. Two years later he was granted a pardon of his acts of piracy by the English government!

YOUR TURN

The history of our world has been shaped by many events—including monster storms. From the sinking of military fleets to the disappearance of large passenger ships, no culture has been safe from nature's fury. Use print and online resources to research a maritime disaster caused by a monster storm. Share what you learn with classmates as either a written report, poster session, or multimedia presentation. Be sure to use maps and models in your presentation.

The Plot Condenses
Air and Water

> "Extreme weather events have such a significant impact on people. I think it's important that we do everything we can to learn more about weather."
>
> —Robbie Hood
> **Atmospheric Scientist, NASA**

Robbie Hood

Robbie Hood is a NASA scientist who uses airplanes and satellites to study rainfall in tropical storms and hurricanes.

Meet the Researchers Video
Learn how Robbie studies hurricanes using airplanes and satellites.

Atmospheric Scientist, NASA

Read more about Robbie Hood online in the JASON Mission Center.

Photos above (left to right): National Geographic; NOAA Photo Library/National Weather Service; Peter Haydock, The JASON Project; Zachari Hauri.

Your Mission...

Pursue energy through the intricate pathways of the water cycle as it fuels monster storms.

To accomplish your mission successfully, you will need to

- Understand the molecular structure of air.
- Investigate the structure of the atmosphere.
- Define the phases and phase changes of water.
- Describe the water cycle.
- Explain how clouds are indicators of upcoming weather.
- Know how dew and fog form.
- Tell how dew point and humidity indicate the amount of water vapor in the atmosphere.

Join the Team

Host Researcher Robbie Hood shows Argonaut Alumnus Liz Quintana a passive microwave detector that she uses to measure water and ice in hurricanes and other storms. The same instrument is mounted on a NASA ER-2 plane and NASA satellites that measure hurricane intensity using rainfall and ice formation as indicators of storm strength. In the future, satellites may be the primary source of storm data collection, eliminating the need for research planes to fly above or even through a storm.

Photo by Peter Haydock, The JASON Project

Background: Scientific Visualization Studio/NASA Goddard Space Flight Center

The Plot Condenses

Imagine flying into a hurricane! Most people might think that would be a bit extreme. However, flying directly into monster storms is business as usual for Robbie Hood. It is her commute to her science laboratory. Robbie Hood is a NASA scientist who studies hurricanes. Unlike her colleagues with both feet on the ground, she does not work within the confines of a laboratory with four walls. Robbie works in the field—actually, she works in the air.

Her mission is to fly into the spiral storm clouds of hurricanes. There, using onboard instruments and electronic packages dropped into the storm, she collects and studies weather data.

Of special interest to Robbie is the rain that falls in these storms. She uses the data she collects to analyze the strength of weather events. Gaining a better understanding of these storms, she can assist other forecasters in making more accurate predictions about hurricanes.

Whether flying missions from Costa Rica, Cape Verde, or airstrips in the Caribbean, Robbie compares the data she and her team collect with data collected by NASA's Earth Observing System of satellites. Satellites such as Aqua have instruments that use different parts of the electromagnetic spectrum to measure water and water vapor. Robbie uses the satellite data to tell how much water is in a particular region of the storm. To obtain more detail, she then compares satellite data with data from the same instruments onboard the research flights. The comparison allows her to better calibrate the satellite's data, which can then provide more reliable information, even when no plane is available to fly into a storm.

Strap in for a mission to explore the dynamics of air and water. In this mission you will investigate the structure of air, the water cycle, and what clouds can tell us about weather.

 Mission 2 Briefing Video See how Robbie uses her knowledge of the atmosphere, the water cycle, and the transfer of energy to understand hurricanes and other storms.

NASA Kennedy Space Center (NASA/KSC)

▲ Crew members prepare for a mission aboard a NASA DC-8 airplane that flies into hurricanes.

Mission Briefing

The Physical Structure of Air

Fan yourself with your hand. Feel that? Something is striking your face, but you cannot see what it is. That invisible substance is air. But what exactly is air, and what is its structure?

Air, like all matter, consists of atoms and molecules. Because air is a gas, these atoms and molecules are not packed as tightly together as they would be in a solid or liquid. In fact, air is about 800 to 900 times less dense on average than solids or liquids. The average **density** of seawater, for example, is 1027 kg/m^3, whereas the average density of air at sea level is 1.2 kg/m^3. This difference means that there is 855 times more matter in one cubic meter of seawater than in one cubic meter of air.

The atoms and molecules in air are constantly moving. As they move, they spread out and mix evenly, ensuring that the atoms and molecules form a single, well-mixed substance.

All gases and gas mixtures, like air, lack a definite shape. If you have ever played with a balloon, blowing it up, twisting it or squeezing it, you have observed this important property of air. Like a liquid, a gas will always take on the shape of its container. This property allows air to move around Earth wherever the wind pushes it. This also makes it possible for convections to develop within weather systems.

The other important characteristic of air is that it lacks a definite volume. By reducing the volume of a parcel of air, you increase its pressure, and by increasing the volume of a parcel of air, you reduce its pressure. Atoms and molecules of air will fill the volume they are given.

Air's lack of shape and indefinite volume, combined with the uneven heating of Earth, produce high- and low-density parcels of air. These parcels are known as high and low pressure areas in the atmosphere. Air moves from areas of higher density (higher pressure) to areas of lower density (lower pressure). It is the expansion, contraction, and movement of air from areas of high density to areas of low density that produces wind.

The Physical Structure of the Atmosphere

Scientists who study the air recognize that it has different characteristics at different altitudes throughout the **atmosphere.** Understanding that the atmosphere isn't uniform around the globe helps them study and understand how weather develops. Scientists have identified four distinct layers of Earth's atmosphere. Take a moment to study the various parts of the diagram below. The two lowest layers of the atmosphere are the most important for the study of weather. These layers are called the **troposphere** and the **stratosphere.**

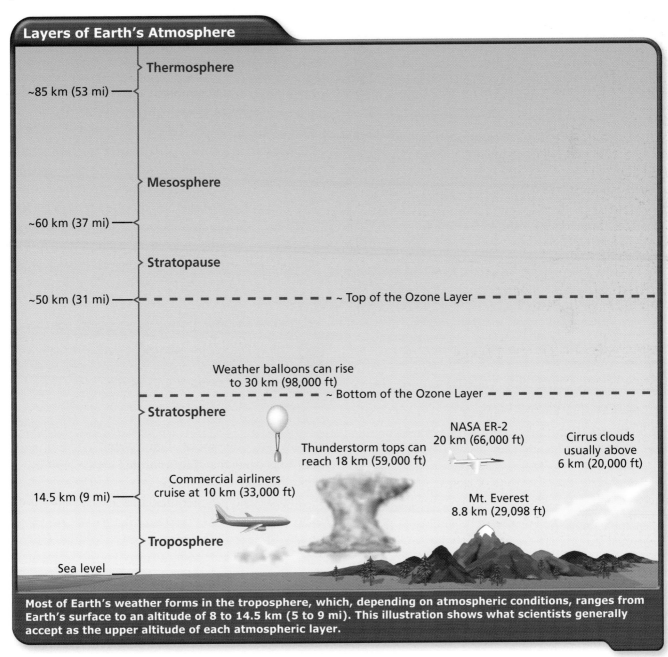

Layers of Earth's Atmosphere

Thermosphere

~85 km (53 mi)

Mesosphere

~60 km (37 mi)

Stratopause

~50 km (31 mi) — ~ Top of the Ozone Layer

Weather balloons can rise to 30 km (98,000 ft)

~ Bottom of the Ozone Layer

Stratosphere

NASA ER-2 20 km (66,000 ft)

Thunderstorm tops can reach 18 km (59,000 ft)

Cirrus clouds usually above 6 km (20,000 ft)

Commercial airliners cruise at 10 km (33,000 ft)

Mt. Everest 8.8 km (29,098 ft)

14.5 km (9 mi)

Troposphere

Sea level

Most of Earth's weather forms in the troposphere, which, depending on atmospheric conditions, ranges from Earth's surface to an altitude of 8 to 14.5 km (5 to 9 mi). This illustration shows what scientists generally accept as the upper altitude of each atmospheric layer.

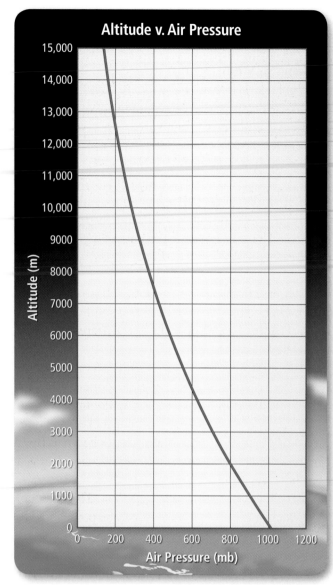

Altitude v. Air Pressure

Altitude (m) / Air Pressure (mb)

Altitude v. Average Humidity

Air Pressure (mb) / Relative Humidity (%) / Altitude (m)

▲ These three graphs show the relationship of altitude to air pressure, average humidity, and average temperature as measured by atmospheric researchers.

The layer of atmosphere closest to Earth is the troposphere, starting at Earth's surface and extending 8 to 14.5 km (5 to 9 mi) high. Look at the graphs on this page and identify the part of each one that represents the troposphere. The troposphere is where the most air, water, and water vapor mix to produce our weather.

The layer just above the troposphere is the stratosphere, extending to about 50 km (31 mi). Find the part of each graph that shows a portion of the stratosphere. Together, the troposphere and stratosphere contain 99 percent of the air in Earth's atmosphere. Between these two layers, temperature and humidity change dramatically. Earth's weather occurs in the troposphere, and its boundary with the stratosphere keeps storms from

growing upward indefinitely. Often, this boundary can be inferred by the anvil-shaped cloud at the top of a thunderstorm.

Scientists have determined a set of average atmospheric conditions for the air within the troposphere. They compare local measurements with these averages. The comparison helps them understand what the weather may do. Let us look at how air pressure, temperature, and the amount of water vapor in the troposphere change on average as you ascend. Changes from these averages help scientists predict changes in the weather.

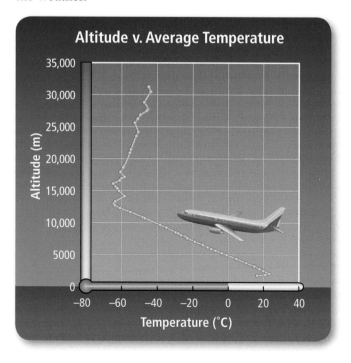

Altitude v. Average Temperature

Altitude (m) / Temperature (°C)

First, consider air pressure. As altitude increases, gravity exerts less pull on the atoms and molecules of air. In addition, there are fewer atoms and molecules "pushing down" from above. As a result, air pressure decreases as you ascend.

A second condition to consider is air temperature. Air temperature tends to decrease with increasing altitude in the troposphere. Air near Earth is warmed by the transfer of heat from Earth's surface and begins to rise. As it rises it loses heat and its temperature decreases. At some point, this warm surface air that is rising and cooling begins to sink. This produces a cycle of rising and falling air, setting up convection currents in the atmosphere. If enough heat is released in this cycle, strong storms can develop.

Finally, humidity tends to decrease as altitude increases. This is because air at Earth's surface is warmer and has more energy to maintain water in its gaseous form.

Phase Changes of Water

Any change in a solid, liquid, or gas to another physical state is called a **phase change.** A phase change always involves a transfer of energy but not a change in chemical composition. Scientists who do

weather research look closely at the phase changes of water. On Earth, water can exist as a solid, a liquid, or a gas. The three states of water have different physical properties.

In its solid state, water exists as ice. As ice absorbs heat energy, its particles begin to vibrate faster. If enough heat energy is added, they will vibrate so violently that they "break free" of their locked position. When this happens, individual particles begin to flow. We observe a phase change from solid to liquid. It is a common transformation called **melting.**

In the liquid state, water particles flow. This freedom of movement gives water its ability to be poured and to take the shape of its container. Although the liquid state of water can change shape, its particles are restricted to a fixed volume. That condition, however, can change if additional heat energy is added to water.

When liquid water gains sufficient heat energy, its particles enter the gas state. This phase change is called **evaporation.** As a gas, the individual particles are not restricted to a mostly sideways flow. Instead, they can spread up and out to fill a container. They can also scatter among the mixture of gases that make up the atmosphere. If conditions are right, the water in solid ice can change directly into water vapor. This process is called **sublimation.**

Water can also undergo changes when heat energy is removed or released. If enough heat energy is removed from water vapor, it becomes a liquid. This phase change is called **condensation.** If enough heat energy is removed from liquid water, it becomes ice. This phase change is called **freezing.** Snow and frost form when water vapor changes directly to a solid state. This process is called **deposition.**

▼ In this view of Riggs Glacier at Muir Inlet in Alaska, you can see water visible as clouds, frozen ice and snow, and liquid ocean.

NOAA Photo Library

The Water Cycle

Water circulates continuously through Earth's crust, oceans, and atmosphere. The physical movement of water in all its physical states, including a complex series of phase changes below, on, and above Earth's surface is called the **water cycle**. It is a process that has been cycling on our planet for billions of years!

Two things stand out when following the water cycle: the formation of fresh water from salt water and the transfer of energy using water.

About 96.5 percent of Earth's water is salt water found in oceans, seas, bays, saltwater lakes, and some groundwater. One of the distinguishing differences between the water from these saline sources and the water found in freshwater lakes, rivers, streams, and even ice and snow is the amount of salt each contains.

If you were to analyze the physical makeup of ocean water, you would find that about 3.5 percent of the weight of the water is salt. In fresh water less than 0.5 percent of the weight is salt. Even fresh water usually contains a small amount of salt.

Fresh water is formed by the evaporation of water from saltwater bodies. As evaporation occurs, the salt is left behind in the ocean or sea. Fresh water, in the form of water vapor, is transported into the atmosphere.

Solar radiation striking the ocean warms the surface water. Individual water particles gain energy and evaporate. Along with other warmed air particles, they spread out, forming an air mass of low density. This warmed, low-density air mass rises. As it gains altitude, the air cools and contracts. Eventually, the rising air cools to a temperature at which its water vapor

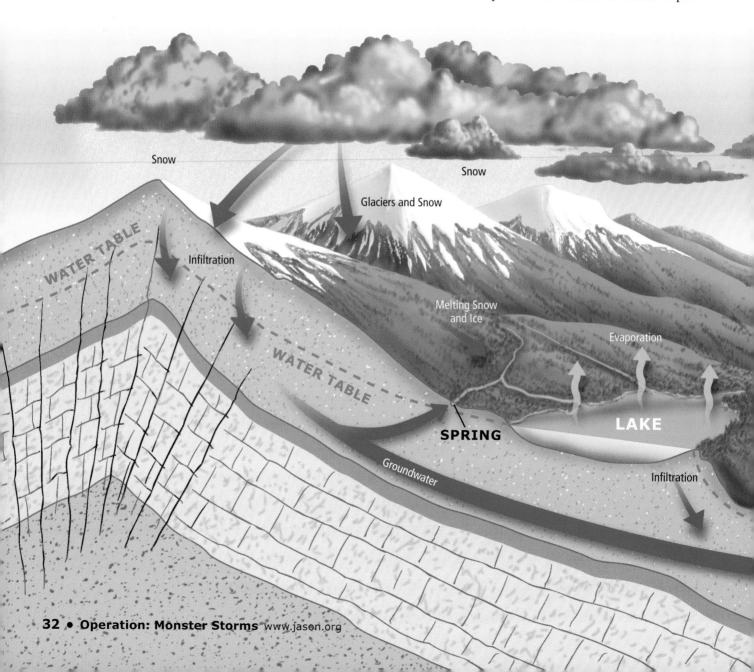

changes state to ice crystals and liquid water, which then become visible as clouds. The water remains aloft until it falls back to Earth as precipitation.

Most precipitation falls over Earth's oceans, simply because oceans cover about 70% of our planet's surface. Precipitation that falls over land masses is our primary source of fresh water. Fresh water can flow along the surface into streams and rivers, or beneath the surface as groundwater. Eventually, most water, moving on a downward slope with the aid of gravity, reaches the oceans. There, the water cycle repeats as solar energy once again warms and evaporates surface water.

In fact, there are many ways that water can circulate through the water cycle by means of other sub-cycles. Water may return directly to the ocean after evaporating. Fresh water may also evaporate and return to the atmosphere without reaching the ocean. Each process is important to how weather develops and changes.

Fast Fact

Although your last drink of water tasted fresh, it may have contained water molecules that rained down on dinosaurs living millions of years ago.

Scientists still do not know exactly where all the water on Earth came from. What they do know is that water started accumulating on our planet in its early history and has played an important role in shaping weather events and climate on Earth. Earth's water cycle is a closed system, with virtually no new water entering or leaving this system.

▼ Solar radiation drives the water cycle, a dynamic process in which water changes state and circulates through Earth's crust, oceans, and atmosphere.

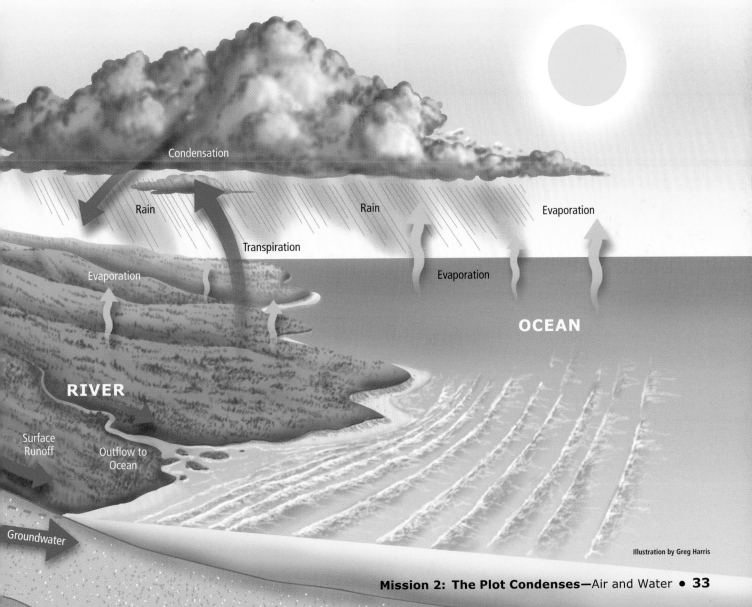

Condensation

Rain

Rain

Evaporation

Transpiration

Evaporation

Evaporation

OCEAN

RIVER

Surface Runoff

Outflow to Ocean

Groundwater

Illustration by Greg Harris

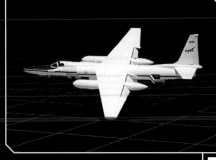
maximum strength of the storm. She needs to know how much water the atmosphere can absorb and what it is most likely to do as the storm develops.

Right now, many of the instruments Robbie uses are mounted in specially outfitted airplanes, like the ER-2, that fly high above the weather events she monitors. In addition, some of these same instruments are on satellites like NASA's Aqua. As Robbie refines and improves the interpretation of the data collected from the planes, this also improves the analysis she can do with the satellite data. This will allow her and other researchers to monitor the atmosphere continuously by satellite and gather data well beyond the locations where they are performing actual research flights.

▼ Most of the fresh water on Earth's surface is not in the liquid state. It is frozen and stored, mostly within the ice cap atop Antarctica. Like its liquid counterpart, this water is also a part of the water cycle. Unlike liquid water that can evaporate quickly, however, water stored in Antarctic ice may need thousands or even millions of years to be recycled.

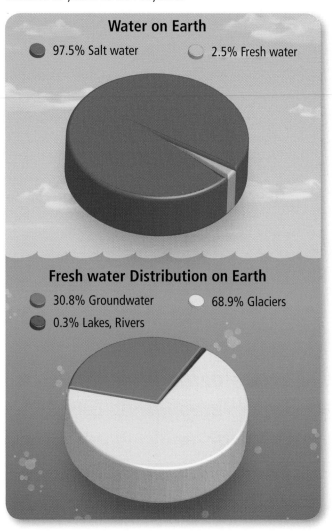

Water on Earth

- 97.5% Salt water
- 2.5% Fresh water

Fresh water Distribution on Earth

- 30.8% Groundwater
- 68.9% Glaciers
- 0.3% Lakes, Rivers

With all of this water cycling around, a lot of energy is being transferred throughout the atmosphere. The water cycle drives both local weather and climatological patterns everywhere on Earth. There are regions of the planet where energy is absorbed more readily and places where it can be released more readily too. Forecasters spend a great deal of time trying to predict the time and location of these phase changes and the precipitation events that can result. We call these precipitation events storms; and the more energy that is released, the bigger the storm. Perhaps some may even form monster storms.

Scientists like Robbie Hood want to understand how water, in the form of liquid water and ice, behaves in hurricanes and other storms. The water cycle can tell her where the water is before the hurricane develops and how it might influence the development and

Energy and the Water Cycle

Robbie Hood uses her understanding of how the water cycle works on Earth to study monster storms. Recently, Robbie and her colleagues began an intense study of water cycles within hurricanes. They are using the ER-2 aircraft and satellites to explore water vapor, water, and ice within the convection of a hurricane.

NOAA Photo Library

If the total amount of water on Earth has changed very little over the past billion years, where does it all go? In this lab, you will see how water can move through a cycle and what happens to the energy as water changes phase.

Materials
- **Lab 1 Data Sheet**
- **clear plastic or glass mixing bowl, medium or large**
- **clean gravel (up to 3-cm-diameter rocks)**
- **large rock**
- **small plastic cup (yogurt or pudding cup)**
- **water**
- **salt**
- **clear kitchen plastic wrap**
- **cotton balls**
- **large rubber bands**
- **dark colored paper or brown paper towels**

Lab Prep
Using the materials provided, build a model of the water cycle that will show evaporation, condensation, and precipitation. In your model you must have a "mountain" and an "ocean." Your ocean must contain salt water. Follow these steps to build your model.

1. Place the plastic cup in the bottom of the mixing bowl and anchor it with enough small rocks inside so that it will not float when water is added later to the bowl. Add gravel to the bowl to produce a mound around the outside of the cup. This is your "mountain."

2. Make a saltwater mixture and add it to the bowl, being careful to keep the water level below the rim of the cup. This is your "ocean."

3. Cover the bowl with plastic wrap. If necessary, use rubber bands to secure the plastic wrap to the rim of the bowl.

4. Position the large rock on top of the plastic wrap, so that it is suspended directly above the plastic cup that sits inside the bowl. You can cover the rock with the cotton balls to simulate a cloud.

5. Place the model in sunlight for at least a day and then observe the results.

Make Observations

1. What purpose does placing your model in the sunlight serve?

2. Describe the parts of your model that illustrate the evaporation and the condensation processes.

3. What happened to the water after it condensed?

4. How did the plastic wrap act as the cold air in your "atmosphere"?

5. What do you think would happen if you covered the bottom of the container with small plants and put the bowl in the sun? How would that change your results?

6. Using two sheets of brown paper towel, soak one in the water that collects in the cup, and one in the water from the bowl. Let both towels dry and observe their appearance. What can you conclude about the salt content in the two water sources?

7. In what ways did this activity accurately represent the water cycle?

Journal Question
Considering the concern over global warming and the human contribution to it, what can we do to lower the amount of greenhouse gases released into the atmosphere? How could you find more information? How could you inform others of what you find?

Photo by Peter Haydock, The JASON Project

▲ By studying the different forms of clouds that are visible, scientists can infer what is happening with water and energy in the atmosphere above.

How Energy and Water Interact in the Atmosphere

The phase changes of water are governed by the flow of heat energy between water molecules and their surroundings. When water molecules in the atmosphere absorb or release enough heat energy, a phase change occurs that strongly influences the type of weather we experience. The phases of water we observe with weather are: the solid phase, ice (sometimes seen as snow, sleet, or hail); the liquid phase, water; and the gaseous phase, water vapor.

If water in the atmosphere is only absorbing energy, we will not see any cloud formation or precipitation nearby. Clouds form when water vapor releases energy to the atmosphere, changing state to ice crystals and liquid water droplets, which we then observe as clouds. When water is absorbing and then releasing a lot of energy in the atmosphere, a storm may soon develop.

Phase Change from Liquid to Gas

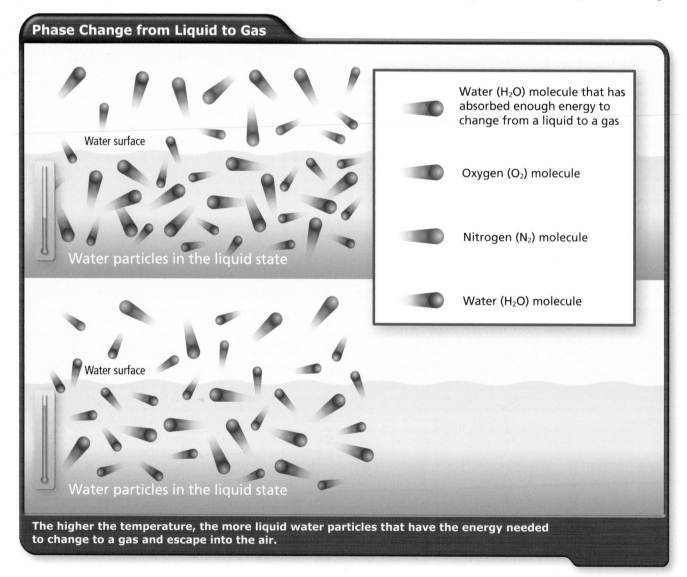

Water surface

Water particles in the liquid state

Water (H₂O) molecule that has absorbed enough energy to change from a liquid to a gas

Oxygen (O₂) molecule

Nitrogen (N₂) molecule

Water (H₂O) molecule

Water surface

Water particles in the liquid state

The higher the temperature, the more liquid water particles that have the energy needed to change to a gas and escape into the air.

▲ Fog forms when water vapor condenses close to the ground.

The perfect conditions for a monster storm occur when a massive and continual supply of heat energy gets carried into the atmosphere by water vapor on convection currents from the surface of the ocean or land. This upward-moving warm air collides with cooler air, which allows the water vapor to transfer its energy into the atmosphere and form storm clouds. With a continuing supply of energy-laden water vapor moving up, the upper-level air parcel is forced to circulate downward to complete the convection. If this process occurs over a large geographic area, it can form tropical storms and hurricanes over the open ocean, or thunderstorms, supercells, or tornadoes over land.

The energy that drives these phase changes originates from the sun. Through the transfer of energy, Earth is kept warm by the sun, and this input of energy drives our water cycle and weather. Natural energy transfer processes on Earth therefore involve the absorption of energy from the sun, the retention of energy with the help of water and other greenhouse gases, and the eventual dissipation of energy back into space. It is the constant inflow of new energy from the sun that keeps driving the water cycle and other atmospheric processes, and keeps Earth livable for us.

The next time you look skyward, you will not actually see the transfer of energy happening, but you can certainly see the results. Watch the clouds—or even the lack of clouds—and you will have a pretty good indicator of the atmospheric processes happening far above you. As you watch clouds form or dissipate, imagine the phase changes of water that are happening in the air and try to follow the transfer of energy going on in the atmosphere.

Fast Fact

Up to 90% of all water in a hurricane may spend at least some of its time frozen within the storm. In fact, at any given time, up to 65% of the water in a hurricane is in a solid ice phase.

Understanding Clouds

Have you ever been in a rainstorm under a cloudless sky? Of course not! That is because it is clouds that act as an overhead reservoir, storing the water that will fall as precipitation.

▲ Cirrus clouds occur above 5500 m (18,055 ft) and indicate fair weather, but may warn of coming precipitation.

Within a cloud, water collects as either ice crystals or liquid droplets. Most condensation or deposition occurs on small particles of smoke or dust. These specks offer a surface on which water vapor can collect as it changes from a gas to a liquid or a solid. These phase changes begin with the formation of microscopic droplets or ice crystals. As water vapor continues to release energy, the ice crystals and water droplets become large enough to be seen and produce the distinct appearance of a cloud.

Although the smallest droplets can be kept aloft by winds within the clouds, the larger droplets are too heavy to remain in the sky. Gravity overcomes any air updrafts, and the droplets fall in some form of precipitation.

▲ Altocumulus clouds are often arranged in parallel layers occurring between 2000 m (6560 ft) and 5500 m (18,055 ft).

Clouds are good indicators of upcoming weather. Their formation and changes can tell us what type of weather to expect. This kind of forecasting does not require high-tech tools. All you need are your eyes. To make your own weather forecasts, look at the sky each day. Note the types of clouds you see. Then, note the kind of weather that follows the appearance of those clouds. Over time, you will see connections between cloud types and upcoming weather.

As you will discover, each type of cloud is often associated with a particular type of weather. Refer to the cloud chart on the next page as you read the descriptions that follow.

▲ Light rain sometimes falls from stratocumulus clouds that form below 2000 m (6560 ft).

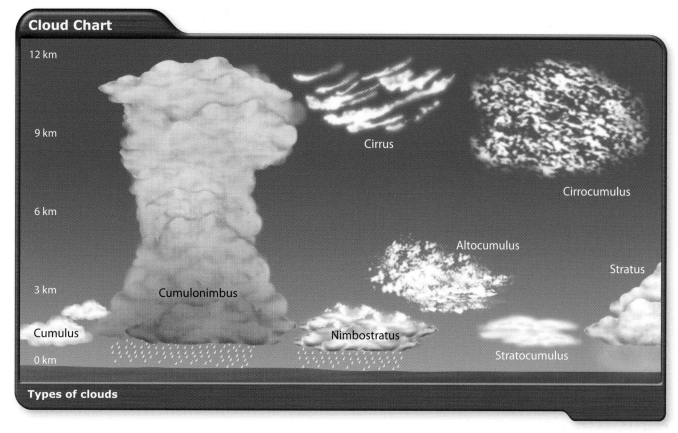

Cloud Chart

12 km

9 km

6 km

3 km

0 km

Cirrus

Cirrocumulus

Altocumulus

Stratus

Cumulonimbus

Cumulus

Nimbostratus

Stratocumulus

Types of clouds

- High, thin clouds, such as cirrus clouds, usually indicate fair, sunny weather.
- Altocumulus clouds, high, fluffy clouds that look like little pillows arranged in parallel rows, often precede colder weather.
- Darker, more dense nimbostratus clouds may indicate a steady, continuous rain or snow.
- Lighter, less dense stratocumulus clouds often precede precipitation.
- Cumulonimbus clouds are thunderstorm clouds. These dark, towering clouds can reach high into the atmosphere and may bring severe weather.

Scientists such as Robbie Hood are interested in what is happening inside storm clouds. They want to know more about clouds and their ice and liquid water contents. Measuring the amount of ice and water in storm clouds can help scientists infer the potential impact of a hurricane or other major storm.

Fog, Dew, and Frost

Although you may not have realized it, you've probably walked through a cloud! You see, not all clouds form high in the atmosphere. Some clouds form at ground level. These low-lying clouds are called **fog.**

Sometimes, a phase change from a gas to a liquid produces liquid water without clouds. This often occurs at night and in the early morning hours when the ground is chilled. Air that remains in contact with chilled surfaces loses the heat energy that keeps water in its gaseous phase. As a result, some of the water vapor molecules undergo condensation and collect as tiny droplets on leaves, grass, cars, and other surfaces. This liquid is called **dew.**

When surface temperatures drop below freezing, and sufficient water vapor is present in the air, the water vapor will undergo a phase change of deposition and form ice on the surface. Instead of forming liquid dewdrops, a thin coating of **frost** appears.

Fast Fact

Clouds are classified into a system that uses Latin words to describe the cloud's appearance from the ground. Cumulus means heap or pile in Latin. Stratus means to spread out or form a layer. Cirrus means curl of hair. And Nimbus means rain.

MEASURING WATER VAPOR		
Measurement	How it is measured/ example	What is measured
Absolute humidity	mass per volume— $2g/m^3$	mass of water vapor in a volume of air
Relative humidity	ratio— 50 percent	amount of water vapor in a parcel of air compared with how much water vapor the air can maintain as a gas at that temperature
Dew point	temperature— 10°C (50°F)	temperature at which water vapor in air will condense to form liquid water

Measuring Water Vapor in the Air

You know when there is a lot of water vapor in the air—you can feel it. Better yet, you can measure it. Scientists use the word **humidity** to describe how much water vapor is in the air. The amount of water vapor in the air is variable and depends on how much energy the water is absorbing and using to maintain its vapor state. On average, about 2 to 3 percent of the molecules in air are water vapor molecules. The higher the humidity, the higher the concentration of water vapor molecules among all the gases.

Humidity, the amount of water vapor in the air, depends on air temperature and the amount of liquid water available to evaporate into water vapor. As the air temperature rises, more heat energy is available for molecules of liquid water to change phase and become water vapor. This additional energy also allows existing water vapor in the air to maintain its gaseous state.

▼ Robbie Hood prepares to show Argonaut Alumnus Liz Quintana a computer model combining satellite photos and other data from Hurricane Katrina. The model shows how sea-surface temperature in the Gulf of Mexico changed as the hurricane absorbed heat energy from the water.

Humidity is actually indicated in two different ways—as both absolute and relative measurements. **Absolute humidity** is a measure of the mass of water vapor in a volume of air. For example, an absolute humidity of $2 g/m^3$, means that each cubic meter of air contains two grams of water vapor particles mixed in among the other gases. Considering that a typical cubic meter of air has a mass of 1200 g, this example shows very little water vapor, or absolute humidity, as part of the total measure of atoms and molecules in the air.

Relative humidity is a ratio. It compares the amount of water vapor existing in a parcel of air with the maximum amount of water vapor the air could maintain as a gas at that temperature. Thus, when the relative humidity is 50 percent, or the weatherman says that the air is "50 percent saturated," the air contains half the water that it is capable of maintaining in the vapor state at that current temperature.

Be careful however, when discussing relative humidity measurements. After all, these measurements are *relative* to their specific air masses with specific temperatures. Different air temperatures change the amount of water vapor the air can absorb. The potential amount of water that the air can absorb depends on the temperature of the air, and increases as the temperature of the air increases. Measurements of 50 percent relative humidity at two different air temperatures are very different if converted to absolute humidity measurements. The higher air temperature will have a higher absolute humidity measurement.

To avoid confusion, scientists sometimes prefer using a different measurement to indicate the amount of water in the air. The **dew point** is the temperature at which enough energy is removed or given up by the water vapor to cause condensation, or liquid water, to form.

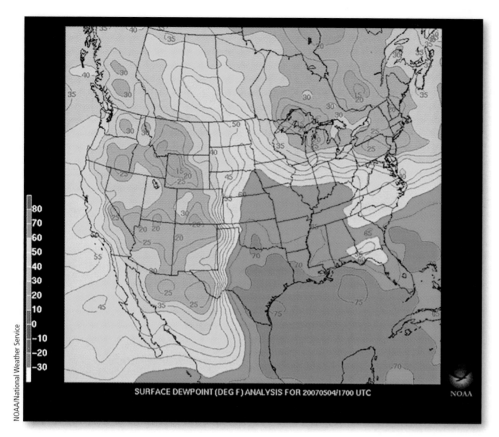

SURFACE DEWPOINT (DEG F) ANALYSIS FOR 20070504/1700 UTC

NOAA

◀ This map shows dew point temperatures across the continental U.S. on the afternoon of May 4, 2007. What do the comparative dew points tell you about how muggy the air might feel in different regions of the country? Extreme changes in dew point over a short distance, as seen over western Texas and eastern Colorado on this map, are an indicator of the potential for severe weather. As this boundary between air masses moved into Kansas later that day, it spawned a series of tornadoes throughout the state. One giant tornado destroyed 95% of the town of Greensburg, Kansas, leaving a path of damage 2.7 km (1.7 mi) wide. The next day, the National Weather Service determined the tornado was a category F-5, among the strongest tornadoes possible (see Fujita Scale on page 57).

Dew point is an important measurement because it tells scientists exactly how much the air temperature needs to cool to form water in some form of condensate, and possibly produce a storm. The closer the air temperature is to the dew point temperature, the more readily a precipitation event will happen.

As you can see, dew point and humidity are very different measurements for describing the amount of water in the atmosphere. Dew point is a temperature. It is measured in degrees and identifies the specific temperature at which water will form from water vapor. This gives more information to a meteorologist to make a weather forecast.

Relative humidity is a percentage. It indicates the amount of water vapor that is in the air, relative to the total amount of water vapor that the air could maintain when totally saturated. Unlike dew point, relative humidity does not identify the temperature at which clouds will form.

Both measurements are valuable, and knowing when to use them is critical to weather forecasters. Relative humidity is most often used to indicate current weather conditions in a single location. Dew point is especially helpful when comparing two locations at the same time for which the air temperatures and water vapor amounts are certain to be different.

Dew point is also the most meaningful measure when talking about the comfort level of the air outside. Some people will begin to feel uncomfortable when the dew point temperature approaches 16°C (60°F). Most people will think the air feels very humid and oppressive when the dew point reaches 21°C (70°F) or higher. When you sweat in hot weather, what makes you feel cooler again? It is the ability of the sweat to evaporate from your skin, that is, for the water on your skin to become water vapor. As dew point increases, your perspiration cannot evaporate as easily, leaving you feeling hot, sweaty, and "sticky." Look at the dew point map above and consider how the air would feel in different regions of the country based on the comparative dew point temperatures.

With the ability to measure water vapor, interpret clouds, and understand the water cycle, scientists can combine this knowledge with satellite, airplane, and radar data to anticipate the threat of a monster storm. Through their research, Robbie Hood and other scientists contribute to saving lives and protecting the property of people who can be affected by hurricanes and other severe storms. Robbie uses her knowledge of the water cycle to study the meaning of the data she collects and understand the clues in the atmosphere. 🌀

Clouds in a Bottle

When Robbie Hood flies into a hurricane or tropical storm to determine its strength and potential impact, she is actually measuring the ice and water content in the storm clouds. The complex and dynamic weather phenomena within the clouds tell Robbie and her team what might happen in the next 12 to 24 hours beneath the storm. But before a monster storm develops, the atmospheric conditions must be right for water vapor to condense into storm clouds and release massive amounts of energy into the atmosphere.

Have you ever wondered what causes a cloud to start forming? Clouds form readily when "seed" particles such as dust or smoke are present in the atmosphere, around which water vapor can condense. In this lab, you will make a model to observe how clouds form, and then analyze the model.

Materials
- Lab 2 Data Sheet
- small plastic bottle with cap (soda or water bottle works well)
- warm tap water
- match

Lab Prep

1. Add 2 cm of warm water to the bottom of the plastic bottle and place the cap back on the bottle. Why do you think water is needed to help form a cloud? Squeeze the bottle several times. What happens? Explain.

2. Remove the cap from your bottle. Your teacher will light a match, blow it out, then drop the smoking matchstick into the bottle. You should cap the bottle as soon as the match is in the water. What do you see?

3. Squeeze the bottle, and then release it. What is happening to the water vapor?

4. Squeeze the bottle again. What happens now? What happens after you release again?

Make Observations

1. Why is the smoke from the match important?

2. What would happen if a lit match were dropped into the bottle? Why do you think this is true?

3. What would happen if you added more water? What would happen if you removed most of the water?

4. What would happen if you used warm water instead of room temperature water? What would happen if you used cold water?

5. What are the similarities between the process of cloud formation and this model? What are the differences?

Journal Question
Now that you know how clouds form, how do you think this knowledge helps Robbie understand monster storms?

▲ Tornadic thunderstorms often produce mammatus clouds like these under their anvil. Aviators avoid these cloud formations because of the likelihood of dangerous wind shear and ball lightning.

Photo by Zachari Hauri

Modeling Atmospheric Signatures

Did you know that every storm has its own signature? Just as your handwriting is different from anyone else's, each storm is slightly different from any other. Water can absorb and emit energy as microwaves. Robbie Hood studies the amount of water in storms and hurricanes by looking at energy emitted by the storm in the form of microwaves.

Water vapor in the atmosphere absorbs heat energy from the ocean's surface. Eventually, that water vapor can contain enough heat energy to start and sustain the convection currents that can develop into a hurricane. By studying this process and the amount of water in the atmosphere for many different storms, Robbie's research helps her and other scientists better predict storm behavior.

Although you cannot duplicate Robbie's research without sophisticated equipment, you can model her research by applying the same principles she uses. In order to understand how weather has been studied over time, you will first use an ancient tool called a hygrometer to measure humidity in the air. Next, you will build a device that models the way Robbie measures the water content in hurricane clouds from a distance. You will then be able to evaluate how far we have come in both our technology and our understanding of the weather.

Photo by Peter Haydock, The JASON Project

Objectives: To complete your mission, accomplish the following objectives:

● Build, calibrate, and use a hair hygrometer.
● Build a model of Robbie Hood's passive microwave instrument.

Materials
- Mission 2 Field Assignment Data Sheet
- hair dryer
- hair hygrometer tool (p. 114)
- calibration sheet
- large white index card or heavy paper
- colored pencils
- squares of blue plastic filters
- tape
- flashlight or other white light source
- unknown samples of filters

Caution! Use caution while operating and handling the hair dryer. Surfaces can become very hot.

Field Preparation

Build and calibrate a hair hygrometer as described on page 114.

1. Design an investigation using your hair hygrometer to examine humidity levels around your home or school. Plan to collect data for at least two weeks. Write out the steps of the procedure that you would follow in your investigation and the purpose of each step.

2. Conduct your investigation and keep a record of your data.

3. Examine your measurements of the amount of humidity around your home or school. What does your hygrometer tell you about the amount of water in the air in your test location?

4. Do your results match your expectations? Why or why not?

5. Do you think this tool is accurate for measuring water in the air? Why or why not?

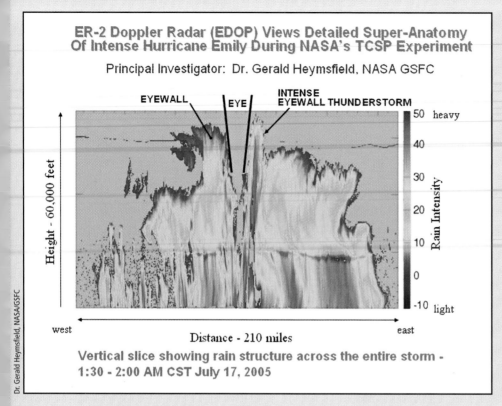

ER-2 Doppler Radar (EDOP) Views Detailed Super-Anatomy Of Intense Hurricane Emily During NASA's TCSP Experiment

Principal Investigator: Dr. Gerald Heymsfield, NASA GSFC

EYEWALL EYE INTENSE EYEWALL THUNDERSTORM

Height - 60,000 feet

Rain Intensity

50 heavy
40
30
20
10
0
-10 light

west east

Distance - 210 miles

Vertical slice showing rain structure across the entire storm - 1:30 - 2:00 AM CST July 17, 2005

Dr. Gerald Heymsfield, NASA/GSFC

◄ This image shows ER-2 Doppler radar data from Hurricane Emily on July 17, 2005. You are looking at a vertical cross-section of the rain bands in the eyewall. Red colors indicate the most intense rain within the hurricane. Dr. Gerald Heymsfield, another NASA hurricane researcher, collected and compiled these data for the hurricane science team.

6 Did you encounter limitations when using this instrument to measure humidity? Explain.

7 Research other designs for a hair hygrometer, and compare and contrast your tool to the others you find. If time permits, build one of the other designs you find and compare the accuracy and precision of your two instruments. Recall that accuracy refers to the correctness of a tool's measurement and precision refers to the tool's ability to consistently repeat the measurement.

Mission Challenge

According to Robbie's studies, the stronger the signal she gets back from the storm, the more water vapor (and therefore energy) is in the air. The more energy there is, the stronger the storm is likely to be. In her studies, Robbie uses microwaves, which are part of the electromagnetic spectrum. Visible light is also part of that spectrum, and because it is easier to measure, we will use visible light to build our model. In this challenge, you will develop your own model sensor to help you determine the amount of "water" in the air and the strength and behavior of your "monster storms."

To set up your model sensor, position the flashlight on a flat surface as shown in the diagram and secure it with tape. Use clay to anchor a 4 × 6 white index card in an upright position on the table, 30 cm (12 in.) away from the front of the flashlight. You will use blue plastic light filters to create your storm "signatures." Before you can read your sensor instrument, however, you will need to calibrate it.

1 To calibrate your instrument, turn on the flashlight and make sure that it is pointing directly at the index card. Cover the light source with one square of the blue plastic filter. What color do you see on the white index card now? Use your colored pencils to illustrate the observed color on your calibration sheet.

2 Add filters to the light source one at a time. Use your colored pencils to record the observed color each time you add a filter, until the observed color is black. Robbie Hood must calibrate her microwave sensor each time she uses it. Would you need to calibrate your instrument each time you use it? Why or why not?

Using your calibration sheet, divide your observed results into 5 sets, numbering them from 1 to 5, with 5 being the darkest set. This will be your intensity scale. Robbie also produces an intensity scale from her calibrations. The scale helps her determine the amount of water in a storm, when she takes her instrument into the field. In your model, the blue filters represent a storm's water content.

③ Your teacher will give you several blue filters taped together in a bundle. You will not know how many layers are in each bundle. Use your calibration sheet to determine the number of filters in each bundle. Assign each bundle an intensity rating from your scale.

④ Now your teacher will give you a series of bundled filters. The series represents the progression of a storm in 24-hour intervals. Use your sensor instrument to assign an intensity rating to each filter bundle. These ratings will represent the storm's water content for each 24-hour period. After you assign an intensity rating to each filter bundle, make a prediction for the intensity rating of the next filter bundle your teacher will give you.

⑤ Record both your predicted and observed intensity rating data in a table and make a chart of time and intensity to tell the story of your storm.

Mission Debrief

① You were asked to predict the strength of a storm based only on the signatures you saw from the previous days. How accurate were you? What other information would have helped you make those predictions?

② How does this represent what Robbie Hood sees when she gathers data using microwave radiation?

③ When you looked at the light source on the paper without any filters, what type of day did that represent (cloudy, clear, rainy, stormy, etc.)? Explain your answer.

④ How much energy do you think is in the atmosphere on a clear day? Explain your answer.

⑤ If water vapor releases heat energy as it rises and condenses, where does that energy go?

⑥ What do the blue filters represent from Robbie Hood's research? The white paper? Explain your answer.

⑦ What do the darker blue colors represent in terms of water vapor in the atmosphere? Explain your answer using Robbie's research methods.

Journal Question Why is Robbie Hood's research important for other scientists who study hurricanes?

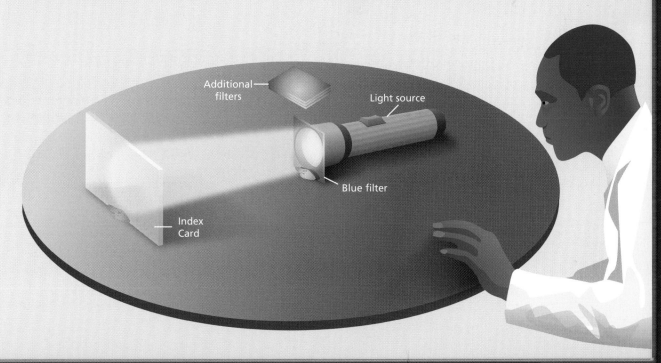

Additional filters

Light source

Blue filter

Index Card

Look up!

It's raining frogs and fish. Impossible, you say?

Definitely improbable. However, there are many recorded events of all sorts of things raining down from the sky.

In June of 2005, residents of Odzaci, a town in Serbia, reported a rainstorm of frogs! According to witnesses, thousands of these tiny amphibians fell from the sky. A similar event was reported in 1997 by a Mexican newspaper. Frogs poured down on the town of Villa Angel Flores.

Stories such as these are not new. In fact, the first reports of these bizarre downpours were recorded thousands of years ago. Over the centuries, there have been all sorts of proposed explanations including religious and supernatural origins for these atypical weather events.

Cola Cans Fall From the Sky!

IOWA–On July 4, 1995, residents of Keokuk, Iowa, found themselves showered in empty soda cans. Apparently a tornado had touched down at a soda bottling plant about 150 miles away. The tornado sucked up soda cans and carried them aloft. As the tornado traveled, it transported them within the winds. Eventually, the winds died down. Once the weight of the cans overcame any lift produced by the whirlwind weather, the cans fell to the ground.

Today, however, many scientists believe that these atypical rains can be explained by more ordinary circumstances. They believe a tornado or a waterspout (tornado over water) moves over a body of water or wetland that is populated by fish, frogs, and other animals. The whirling winds suck up the unfortunate animals, carrying them aloft. As the tornado moves, it transports its passengers away from their habitat. As the tornado dissipates, the winds lack sufficient energy to keep their living load aloft. Gravity takes over and the animals fall to Earth, deposited in a new and often dry environment.

Sometimes, the updrafts are strong enough to transport the unlucky passengers into the frigid air of upper altitudes. There, the water content of the animals freezes, producing rock-hard projectiles.

Some scientists suggest that these frozen animals get trapped in an atmospheric cell that is associated with hail formation. Within this continual up-and-down movement, multiple layers of ice are added, completely burying the animals in the centers of hailstones.

Your Turn

Back in 1921, after examining reports of odd rainstorms, a fish biologist published a paper entitled "Rains of Fishes." In it, he offered four possible explanations for the appearance of fish scattered over the landscape following a rainstorm.

a. The fish had adaptations to slip-and-slide over wet land and therefore had not fallen from the sky. Instead they were migrating from pond to pond.

b. Ponds and lakes had overflowed and deposited the fish in the roads.

c. Fish that were buried and in a state of "hibernation" were awakened by the heavy rainstorms.

d. A tornado, whirlwind, or waterspout had sucked up the animals and carried them over land. As the winds died down, the transported animals fell from the sky.

Suppose you arrived at a town in which fish had been discovered over the landscape following a rainstorm. What happened?

1. Design a strategy for inquiry that would address each of the above proposed explanations, a–d.

2. Propose additional explanations for this odd discovery. Make sure to include a strategy for inquiry that would test your proposed explanation against the facts.

The Chase
On the Run in Tornado Alley

> *"I study the bottom 30 feet of the tornado because that is the area that impacts us the most and the area we know the least about."*
>
> **—Tim Samaras**
> **National Geographic Emerging Explorer**

Tim Samaras

Tim Samaras and his research team have designed probes that can survive tornadoes. Every May and June, Tim uses these probes to collect important tornado data.

 Meet the Researchers Video
Discover what motivates Tim and how he chases tornadoes across Tornado Alley.

National Geographic Emerging Explorer ▢ NATIONAL GEOGRAPHIC

 Read more about Tim online in the JASON Mission Center.

Photo by Peter Haydock, The JASON Project

Your Mission...

Alert your community to the threat of thunderstorms and tornadoes by tracking the elusive clues in the atmosphere.

To accomplish your mission successfully, you will need to

- Explain thunderstorm formation.

- Understand how lightning and thunder form in a storm.

- Describe how a tornado forms within a thunderstorm.

- Detail why tornadoes are so common in Tornado Alley.

- Recognize the importance of dew point in thunderstorm and tornado development.

- Research the tools used to forecast and study tornadoes.

- Predict the threat of severe weather in your community.

Join the Team

These Argonauts are chasing tornadoes with Tim Samaras! First, the Argonauts collect critical weather data showing where tornado-producing storms could strike. Next, they venture into the field to deploy Tim's data-collecting probes. The weather measurements they collected confirm that Denver would see storms in the afternoon. Here, the Argos use time-lapse photography and observe the storm formation they predicted. Clockwise, from top left: Host Researcher Tim Samaras, Student Argonaut Matheus DeNardo, Teacher Argonaut John Hartman, Student Argonaut Jing Fan, and Student Argonaut Amanda Stucke.

Photo by Jude Kesl

On the Run in Tornado Alley

With a rumble and roar as loud as a freight train, a monster tornado approaches your position. As the tornado nears, you hastily place atmospheric and video probes in its path. Then, you and your storm-chaser team jump into a van and flee the scene. From a safe distance you watch the tornado pass directly over the probes. When it is safe to go back, you rush to collect the probes and the valuable data they have recorded.

If you can see yourself in this scene, you have an idea of what it would be like to ride along with researcher Tim Samaras as he chases storms across Tornado Alley. Tim tries to predict where a tornado might occur and then rushes to that location to study the developing storm. He uses weather maps, the Internet, and weather data such as dew point and temperature to identify where the storms are most likely to form. Once there, Tim and his team attempt to deploy probes in the path of any tornado that forms. The probes record air pressure, temperature, humidity, wind speed, and the direction in which the tornado is moving.

One of Tim's most dramatic tornado encounters occurred in June 2003 in the town of Manchester, South Dakota. The tornado packed winds estimated at 418 km/h (260 mph) and was approximately 0.8 km (0.5 mi) wide. Tim's probes collected amazing data. As the tornado passed over, the probes recorded the largest weather-related drop in air pressure ever measured.

Tim helps scientists better understand tornadoes. His work may help tornado forecasters more accurately predict where and when tornadoes could form. Tim hopes that such predictions will help save lives and protect homes and property.

Like Tim, you are about to take on a mission. You will learn how to collect weather intelligence, forecast severe weather, and predict the threat of tornadoes in your community.

 Mission 3 Briefing Video Prepare for your mission by viewing this briefing on your objectives, and see an introduction to thunderstorm and tornado science.

Mission Briefing

Thunderstorm Formation

Thunderstorms form as warm, moist air rises. This upward movement of air can result from surface heating. Areas that are heated by sunlight transfer some of this energy to the air that is directly above. As the air warms, it becomes less dense and starts to rise.

Air can also rise due to the arrival of a cold front. Because cooler air is more dense than warmer air, cooler air "hugs" the ground and can act as a wedge. As it collides with the warmer air mass, it pushes the warm air skyward. The ascending air forms and fuels the towering clouds of a thunderstorm. A system such as this can spawn strong winds, lightning, heavy precipitation, and even tornadoes.

▲ The atmospheric data instruments in one of Tim's probes record data directly from a passing tornado.

The upward movement of air acts like a conveyor belt. The atoms and molecules that make up the air are transported skyward, carrying energy into the thunderstorm-generating clouds in the atmosphere. Some of this energy is **kinetic energy**, exhibited by the increased movement of warm air up into the atmosphere. However, most of the energy that fuels thunderstorm formation is **latent heat energy** contained within the **water vapor**—water molecules in their gaseous state—in the rising air.

As water vapor rises into the atmosphere, it releases heat energy when it cools. As a result, the temperature of the water vapor drops. When the temperature of the air decreases to its **dew point**—the temperature at which water vapor condenses into water—water droplets begin to accumulate on tiny particles of dust in the atmosphere, forming a cloud.

During this phase change, water vapor releases its substantial store of latent heat energy, fueling the thunderstorm. The additional energy allows the air to rise high into the **troposphere.** The storm cloud is continually fed with more energy from the updraft of warm, moist air that is rising into it. As air cools high in a thunderstorm, it also begins to descend in some places. These downdrafts can be accompanied by heavy rain and hail. The cycle of rising and descending air forms an atmospheric convection that strengthens the storm.

Eventually, the thunderstorm runs out of the energy it needs to maintain its forceful presence. With its fuel of water vapor transformed into downpours, little

Fast Fact

The average thunderstorm lasts only 30 minutes and is 24 km (15 mi) in diameter. Besides torrential rain, thunderstorms can produce straight-line winds of 160 km/h (100 mph), hail, and tornadoes. The clouds that form a thunderstorm can reach elevations over 17,000 m (55,775 ft). In any given moment, there is an average of 1800 thunderstorms occurring around the world, totaling over 16,000,000 thunderstorms worldwide each year.

energy is left to power storm winds. Without updrafts, the system is further starved of rising and condensing vapor. As the remaining winds weaken, the thunderstorm dissipates.

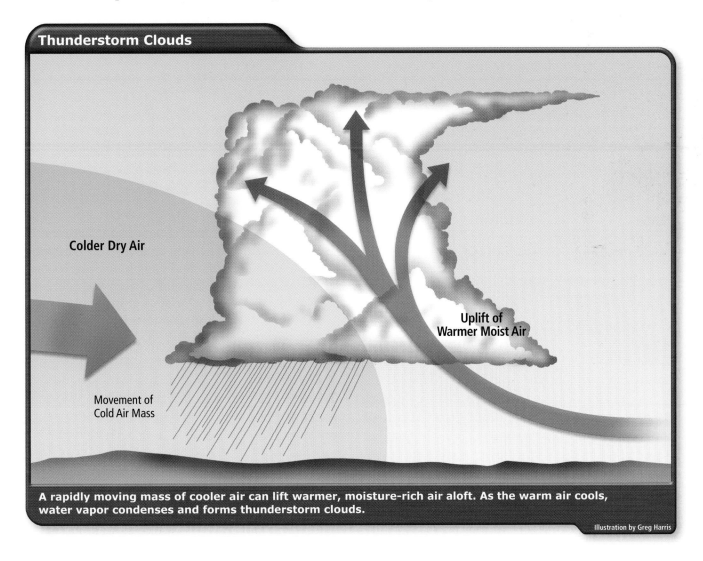

Thunderstorm Clouds

Colder Dry Air

Uplift of Warmer Moist Air

Movement of Cold Air Mass

A rapidly moving mass of cooler air can lift warmer, moisture-rich air aloft. As the warm air cools, water vapor condenses and forms thunderstorm clouds.

Illustration by Greg Harris

It's Not Just the Heat, It's the Dew Point!_____

When looking for tornadoes to chase, Tim Samaras needs to know about dew point. Knowing where high and low dew points exist helps define where severe storms and tornadoes are likely to occur.

Tim uses temperature and dew point data to find a **dry line**, a particular margin between two air masses of different characteristics.

In order for a thunderstorm to form, the air mass ahead of the dry line needs to have plenty of water vapor. This condition is indicated by a high dew point temperature. The air mass behind the dry line needs to have less water vapor. As this drier mass pushes ahead, it acts like a wedge, driving the high dew point air upward. As this vapor-rich air ascends, it cools rapidly and releases its store of energy. It is this energy transported aloft that drives the formation of the powerful storm systems.

In this lab, you will measure dew point to determine the impact this temperature has on weather. In the map shown, air temperatures appear over dew point temperatures, both of which are more commonly recorded in English units (°F) in the United States.

Dry Line Map

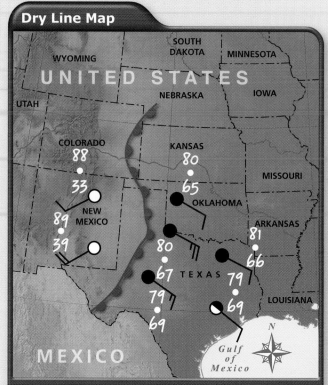

A dry line often appears where dew points east of the line are above 50°F (10°C) with winds from the southeast, and dew points west of the dry line are generally below 40°F (4°C). Air temperatures also can differ east and west of the line. In the spring, temperatures east of the dry line are usually between 70° and 80°F (21° to 27°C), and temperatures west of the line are typically above 85°F (29°C). Tornadic thunderstorms often develop just east of a dry line.

Materials
- **Lab 1 Data Sheet**
- **dew point tool** (p. 114)

Lab Prep

Answer these questions before you go into the field with your dew point tool.

1. Build your dew point tool. Practice measuring the dew point in your classroom several times. Where did the moisture on the outside of the can come from? Did you and your teammates observe the same dew point temperature?

2. From your classroom measurements, what would you say about the water vapor content of your room? Do you have high or low humidity? What could you do to lower the amount of water vapor in your classroom? What could you do to increase it?

3. What is the relationship between dew point and humidity?

4. What is the relationship between the rising of warm, moist air and cloud formation?

5. Research other types of boundaries between air masses. Collectively, these are called **fronts.** Complete the definition table in the Lab 1 Data Sheet for the fronts you research. Indicate and compare the characteristics of the air masses you would expect to see ahead of and behind each front.

Make Observations

1. Use the dew point tool to measure the amount of water in the air in several locations in your school over several days. Before you take measurements, think about and answer these questions:

   a. In which places would you expect to see differences? What characteristics make you think this?

b. What time(s) of day will be best to take measurements? Does time matter? Why?

c. How many times and from how many places do you need to collect data before you can use your findings to make predictions? Discuss this with your mission group to decide your answers. Make sure you can justify your answers to your teacher!

2 Design an experiment using your dew point tool, the data you collected, and a map of the school to determine where dry lines exist.

a. What data, in addition to air temperature and dew point temperature, do you need to collect?

b. Where do you expect to see dry lines?

3 Design an experiment to observe the relationship (if any) between dew point, air temperature, and weather. Observe clouds and make note of the type of weather that occurs before and after temperature and dew point changes.

a. Decide as a class how long the experiment should be conducted.

b. Decide as a class where you should take your measurements and make your cloud cover observations.

c. After collecting your data, discuss changes you observed in the weather and how dew point and air temperature might be related to your observations.

Interpret Data

1 In your school, you probably found dry lines, but you did not find tornadoes. Explain why thunderstorms do not form inside your school. Consider what other weather conditions are necessary for these storms to form.

2 Why might dew point in an area change?

3 If you observed dew point changes, how often did they occur? Why did these changes happen?

4 How does dew point impact your life other than indicating the potential of storm formation?

5 Tornadoes can form near fronts and dry lines. What conditions do each of these boundaries have in common that make the tornado formation possible?

 Journal Question You know that dew point is the temperature at which the air is saturated, and that relative humidity is the percentage of how saturated the air is for a measured air temperature. Why would scientists use dew point, rather than relative humidity, to determine where storms might be found?

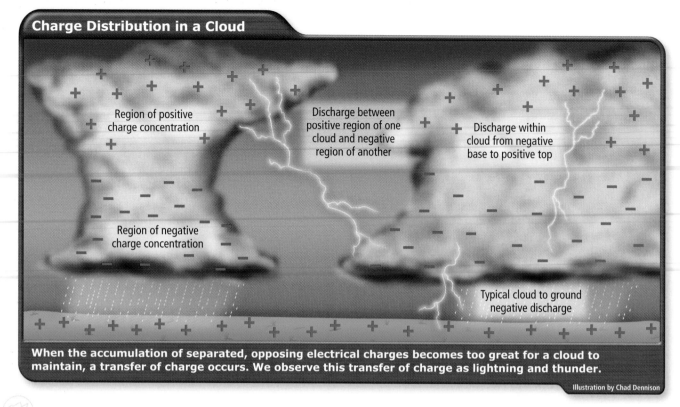

Charge Distribution in a Cloud

Region of positive charge concentration

Discharge between positive region of one cloud and negative region of another

Discharge within cloud from negative base to positive top

Region of negative charge concentration

Typical cloud to ground negative discharge

When the accumulation of separated, opposing electrical charges becomes too great for a cloud to maintain, a transfer of charge occurs. We observe this transfer of charge as lightning and thunder.

Illustration by Chad Dennison

Lightning and Thunder

In addition to wind and heat, most storms produce electrical energy. This energy is generated by the formation and separation of charged particles within the clouds.

When chasing tornadoes, scientists like Tim Samaras look for **lightning** in the storm. Lightning usually occurs ahead of the region in which a tornado is most likely to form. This knowledge helps Tim decide on the best locations for deploying his probes.

Although lightning is a common weather condition, scientists are not sure what causes clouds to become electrified. However, they do know that electrically charged clouds are unstable.

Whirled by winds, positive and negative charges separate and collect in different regions of the cloud. As the cloud's store of electrical energy increases, this separation becomes increasingly unstable. When the separation of opposing electrical charges becomes too great for the cloud to maintain, it releases its stored energy. The release of charged particles races through the air and creates the brilliant flash that we see as lightning.

Lightning takes different forms. The most common discharge never reaches the ground. It does not even leave the cloud in which it forms! These bolts transfer charges between regions of the same cloud and return the cloud to a more stable state.

The next most common lightning surges between clouds and the ground. As electrical charges within a cloud separate, the top of the cloud becomes positive. The bottom takes on a negative charge. This negative charge produces a strong electromagnetic field that upsets the electrical balance of the surrounding air. It also causes the ground beneath the cloud to assume a positive charge.

The unstable state becomes strong enough to overcome the insulating capacity of the air between the cloud and ground. The first stream of negative charge races from the cloud to the ground. Called a stepladder, this small stroke follows a zigzag path. As it nears the ground, a stream of positive charge rises up from the ground. When these two charge flows meet, the circuit is closed. Immediately, a massive stroke of electricity—a lightning bolt— moves between the cloud and ground.

On rare occasions, lightning can even form between clouds. As this major transfer of charge occurs, a bright flash of lightning can be seen in the sky.

Lightning superheats the air around it to temperatures that can exceed the temperatures observed on the surface of the sun. This sudden and extreme change causes the air to expand violently. The expansion produces a shockwave, and the resulting sonic boom we hear and feel is **thunder**.

Distance to a Thunderstorm

When on a chase, Tim Samaras has to know whether a storm is headed toward him or moving away from him—after all, he has to deploy his probes in the right place to collect that elusive tornado data!

You also need to know where storms are, particularly if you are going to be outside when one is brewing. In this lab, you will use the information in the table to determine distance to a thunderstorm. After you are comfortable with determining the distance to a thunderstorm, you will go online to view real thunderstorms and apply what you have learned.

Time Difference Between Lightning and Thunder (seconds)	Distance to Lightning	
	kilometers	miles
1	0.33	0.21
2	0.67	0.42
3	1.00	0.62
4	1.33	0.83
5	1.67	1.04
6	2.00	1.24

Materials
- Lab 2 Data Sheet
- Internet access
- paper and pencil
- stopwatch or a clock with a second hand

 Caution! If you are outside during a storm and you hear thunder, the storm is within 16 km (10 mi) and you could be in danger. Find shelter and wait for 30 minutes after the last thunderclap before going outside. Lightning strikes, on average, kill 80 people and injure over 300 people per year in the United States.

Lab Prep
Use the data in the table above to determine the distance to a thunderstorm.

1. You see lightning hit a hilltop that is 3 km away. About how long will the thunder take to reach you?

2. You see lightning and then hear thunder 14 seconds later. How far away was the lightning?

3. Using the data table above, construct three problems for a classmate to solve. The questions should ask how to determine either the distance to a thunderstorm or the time it will take for you to hear thunder if you know the distance to the lightning strike. Try to use values not listed in the table. Is there a pattern you can use to figure out the answer without the table?

Make Observations
Go to the **JASON Mission Center** and view the *Thunderstorm* video clip. Use data from the table, lightning strikes that you see, and thunderclaps that you hear in the video to determine how far the storm is from the person recording it.

1. What is the distance to the storm at the start of the clip? In the middle? At the end?

Interpret Data
Design a procedure that will allow you to use the lightning strikes seen in the *Thunderstorm* video clip to track the distance to the storm and its relative direction.

1. When is the storm coming toward you or moving away from you? How do you know?

2. What calculations do you need to do?

3. What data do you need to collect to make your calculations?

 Record your procedure, results, and analysis in your JASON Journal.

 Journal Question Tim is doing research to determine how lightning forms. Based on the Mission Briefing you have been reading and the *Connection* article "Lightning: A Monster Transfer of Energy" (pages 106–107), what data must Tim collect to help him solve this mystery?

Tornado Formation Within a Thunderstorm

A portion of a thunderstorm cloud can begin to rotate if winds at different heights above the ground are blowing in different directions. The most hazardous thunderstorms, called **supercells,** have a zone of strong rotation. As the rotation becomes more and more concentrated, a narrow column of rapidly spinning air may develop from the base of the storm. If the column stretches all the way to Earth's surface, it becomes a **tornado**—a violently spinning column of air extending from a thunderstorm cloud and in contact with the ground.

As Tim Samaras's probes have measured, air pressure is very low at the center of a tornado. Air rushes toward the tornado from all directions. As air rises and water vapor condenses inside the tornado, a funnel cloud forms. The lower part of a tornado can become very dark as it picks up dirt and debris. The whirling winds of the strongest tornadoes are estimated to be the fastest winds on Earth. Scientists classify tornadoes by wind speed and the damage they cause. All tornadoes are extremely dangerous.

Tornado Atmospheric Data Probe

The probe is a squat, cone-shaped weather station designed to be placed in the direct path of a tornado. Instruments protected by the tornado-proof shell monitor, collect, and record data from passing twisters.

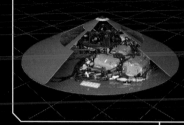

Data Probe Specifications:

Diameter: 50 cm (20 in.); 76 cm (30 in.) for camera-equipped models

Height: 15 cm (6 in.)

Mass: 20 kg (44 lbs); 38.5 kg (85 lbs) for camera-equipped models

Composition: Tornado-proof, steel exterior shell; shatter-resistant plastic windows on models modified for video cameras.

Instrumentation: Weather instruments measure air pressure, temperature, humidity, wind direction, and wind speed. Camera-equipped models: six outward-facing cameras, each captures a 60-degree view of the landscape; one upward-facing camera captures overhead images.

- The squat, cone shape of the probe prevents a tornado's winds from lifting it from the ground.
- The exact placement of a probe arises from Tim Samaras's best guess as to the most likely path of the twister.
- On June 11, 2004, the eye of a tornado passed within 3 m (10 ft) of a video probe, giving its cameras the closest view ever of a twister's center!

Tornadic Thunderstorm

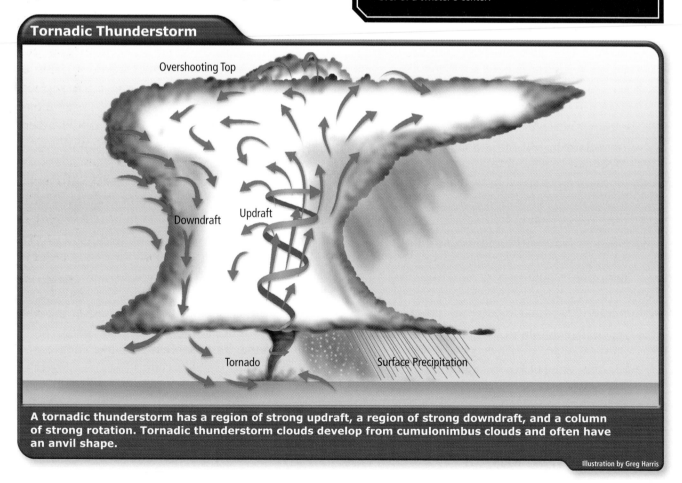

Overshooting Top

Downdraft

Updraft

Tornado

Surface Precipitation

A tornadic thunderstorm has a region of strong updraft, a region of strong downdraft, and a column of strong rotation. Tornadic thunderstorm clouds develop from cumulonimbus clouds and often have an anvil shape.

Illustration by Greg Harris

Enhanced Fujita Scale

Category	Wind Speed	Potential Damage
EF0	105–137 km/h 65–85 mph	Light damage. Peels surface off roofs; some damage to chimneys; branches broken off trees; shallow-rooted trees pushed over; mobile homes pushed off foundations or overturned; sign boards damaged.
EF1	138–179 km/h 86–110 mph	Moderate damage. Roofs torn off frame houses; windows and glass doors broken; moving autos blown off roads; mobile homes demolished; boxcars overturned.
EF2	180–217 km/h 111–135 mph	Considerable damage. Roofs torn off well-constructed houses; foundations of frame homes shifted; large trees snapped or uprooted; light-object missiles generated; cars lifted off ground.
EF3	218–266 km/h 136–165 mph	Severe damage. Some walls torn off well-constructed houses; trains overturned; most trees in forest uprooted; heavy cars lifted off the ground and thrown; structures with weak foundations blown away some distance.
EF4	267–324 km/h 166–200 mph	Devastating damage. Well-constructed houses and whole frame houses completely leveled; structures with weak foundations blown away some distance; trees debarked; cars thrown and small missiles generated.
EF5	>324 km/h >200 mph	Incredible damage. Strong frame houses leveled off foundations and swept away; with strongest winds, brick houses completely wiped off foundations; automobile-sized missiles fly through the air in excess of 100 m (109 yd); cars thrown and large missiles generated; incredible phenomena will occur.

Inferring Tornado Wind Speeds

Here is a riddle. How do you determine the force of something that is powerful enough to destroy the very instruments intended to measure it? Although this seems to be a trick question, it is not. It is a problem that weather scientists face when trying to measure the wind speed of a tornado.

Until the early 1970s, no one agreed on how to measure tornado winds. As a result, tornadoes were not well distinguished from one another. Then in 1971, Professor Tetsuya Fujita demonstrated a way of estimating tornado wind speed by evaluating the damage caused by these powerful whirlwinds. The method is called the **Fujita Scale,** or F-Scale.

The original Fujita Scale was based largely on the extent of damage done to houses and mobile homes, and the effects of high winds on vehicles and trees. The weakest tornadoes, those that had caused minor damage to chimneys and tree limbs, were assigned an F0 rating, or gale tornado status. As the wind speed increased, so did the "F" value. An incredible tornado was assigned a rating of F5. Its impact would be recognized only after the event by evidence such as remnants of strong frame houses that had been carried from their foundations and torn apart.

Although the Fujita Scale offers a way to compare tornado strength, it is subjective. Its reliability and repeatability depend on several factors. First, reliability depends on the skill of the surveyor. Will all surveyors know how to distinguish tornado damage from the downburst of straight-line winds? Will surveyors be consistent in interpreting the extent of damage? In addition to human inconsistency and subjectivity, location can introduce differences as well. Structures and trees vary from place to place, making it difficult to standardize observations. Estimating wind speed in isolated regions where there are no structures to be damaged is also a challenge.

To address these problems, weather experts now use an enhanced Fujita Scale. Known as the **EF-Scale,** this system is expanded to include 28 more diverse and better described damage indicators. This results in less observer bias and more consistency when comparing tornadoes. Familiar locations such as schools, strip malls, high-rise buildings, and warehouses are now included as specific damage indicators. If a tornado passes by one of these structures, the damage done to the building provides information to infer wind speed more accurately.

Although the EF-Scale offers an enhanced means of rating and comparing tornadoes, it remains subject to human bias. Perhaps future technologies will provide a direct and immediate measurement of tornado wind speed. Until then, however, we are limited to inferring the magnitude of these monster winds from the damage they wreak.

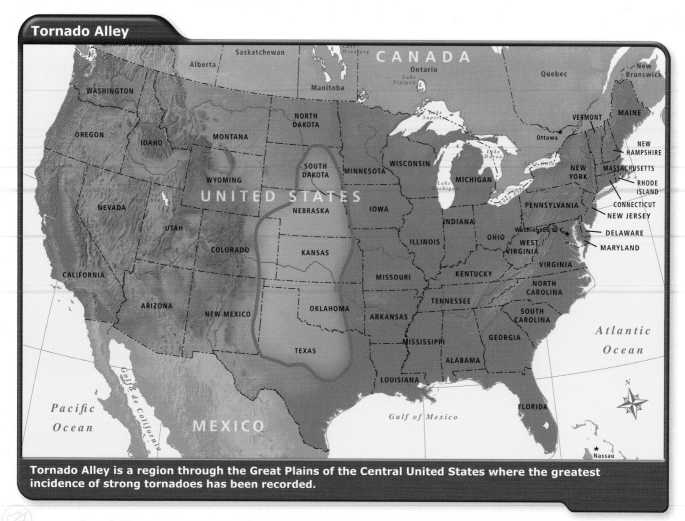

Tornado Alley is a region through the Great Plains of the Central United States where the greatest incidence of strong tornadoes has been recorded.

Tornado Alley

Tornadoes occur all over the world, but conditions in the Great Plains of the United States are particularly favorable for their development. That is why this part of North America is called **Tornado Alley.**

South of Tornado Alley, warm, moist air moves northward from the Gulf of Mexico. At the same time, cooler, drier air that has passed over the Rocky Mountains spills eastward. In Tornado Alley, the two air masses clash. The eastward-moving dry air forces the moist air skyward. As it ascends, the moist air cools below its dew point. Water vapor condenses, releasing energy that fuels the formation of supercells.

Fronts usually define these clashes between air masses. However, another boundary can occur and can form violent storms in spring, when the differences between temperatures and humidity are greatest. This smaller scale boundary, called a **dry line,** occurs when moist, northward-moving air from the Gulf of Mexico meets dry, eastward-moving air from the Rocky Mountains.

Explosive development of thunderstorms can take place when the moist air rises rapidly. One or more of these storms can develop into a supercell that produces a tornado. In rare instances, a large thunderstorm or area of severe thunderstorms can spawn a tornado outbreak, an occurrence of multiple tornadoes within the storm area. The largest tornado outbreak on record, which spawned 148 tornadoes across 13 states and Canada, occurred on April 3–4, 1974. This event is known as the "Super Outbreak."

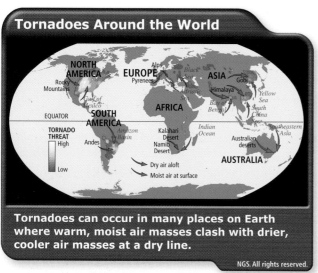

Tornadoes Around the World

Tornadoes can occur in many places on Earth where warm, moist air masses clash with drier, cooler air masses at a dry line.

Modeling Tornadoes

Although Tim Samaras chases tornadoes, he must be careful not to catch one! A tornado's funnel-shaped cloud is a powerful vortex that acts much like the moving air drawn into a home vacuum sweeper. Scientists, however, do not really know what is happening in a storm the instant a tornado starts to form.

In this lab, you will make a model of a tornado in order to observe the structure and impact of a vortex.

NOAA Photo Library/ National Severe Storms Laboratory (NSSL)

Materials
- Lab 3 Data Sheet
- two 8- or 10-oz. tall, clear plastic flat bottom jars with screw caps
- liquid dish soap
- small, light objects such as plastic beads or glitter for "debris"
- water
- flashlight (optional)

Lab Prep

Answer these questions before you make your model.

1. What are some of the conditions that make Tornado Alley an ideal place for tornadoes to form?

2. Scientists use models to help them understand monster weather. Why do you think they use models in addition to observations and direct measurements?

Make Observations

Fill the first jar ¾ full with water. Add some beads or glitter and a drop of liquid soap. Replace the lid and swirl the jar until you see a funnel form. Answer the following questions about your tornado model. Using a flashlight to backlight the jar may help you see the funnel better.

1. What happens to the "debris"?

2. Why does the debris move as it does?

Add water to the second jar, but only ½ of the amount used in the first jar. Add a drop of liquid soap and "debris."

3. Does the amount of water you add to the jar make a difference to how the model operates?

4. What happens when you swirl the jar quickly? Slowly? Is there a difference between the jars?

Now empty your second jar, being careful to save the "debris." Fill the jar ¾ full with clean water, equal to the level of the first jar, but do NOT add liquid soap this time.

5. Compare the first jar that has liquid soap to the second jar without it. Does the soap make a difference in how the model operates?

6. What do you notice when you swirl the jars quickly? Slowly?

7. To model a tornado accurately, is it important to swirl the jar in a particular direction (clockwise or counterclockwise)?

Interpret Data

This activity shows you one way that scientists study weather phenomena—they use models. Models help them see what is happening without actually getting into a tornado. However, models are only as good as the knowledge or data used to make them. Use your data to analyze your model.

1. How does this jar model imitate the formation of a real tornado? How is it different?

2. What could you do to make your model more realistic?

3. How can a model like this help you understand tornadoes?

Journal Question Tim's probes record data near the bottom of the tornado. Why do scientists find such data particularly important?

Tools to Forecast and Study Tornadoes

Maps that show weather conditions are valuable to scientists who study the formation of thunderstorms and tornadoes. A series of such maps can show how conditions change both at ground level and high above the ground. Satellite images and **Doppler radar** displays show almost instantaneously how weather conditions are developing. However, even Doppler radar usually cannot "see" a tornado directly. The tools that scientists and forecasters use can indicate only when conditions *may* be right for a tornado to develop. The National

National Oceanic and Atmospheric Administration (NOAA)

▲ Hook- or comma-shaped echoes in Doppler radar, like the red portion of this image, suggest that a tornado has formed.

▼ Mobile Doppler radar units can be stationed wherever they are needed. These units allow researchers and forecasters to collect tornado data that nonmobile radar could miss.

▲ The most devastating tornado in Wyoming history tore through a Cheyenne trailer park on July 16, 1979.

Weather Service depends on trained tornado spotters to verify whether a tornado has actually formed.

Tim Samaras goes to the Internet for data showing where supercell thunderstorms are likely to develop. Still, even after he locates a storm, he relies on his own observations. He studies the shape and movement of a storm. Then, he decides where to position himself and his team for the best chance of deploying probes in the path of a tornado.

Future Challenges

Many challenges remain in understanding and forecasting tornadoes. Here are some questions yet to be answered:

- Why do some severe thunderstorms produce tornadoes while others do not?
- What is happening inside a storm the instant a tornado starts to form?
- Most tornadoes last for only a few minutes. Why do some last for more than an hour?

Team Highlight

JING FAN
Student Argonaut, Connecticut

On day two, Jing Fan and Tim Samaras set out probes near Bear Creek Lake, outside of Denver, Colorado, to measure wind speed and air pressure within the bottom 9 m (30 ft) of a tornado. It is within this portion of a tornado that we understand its dynamics the least, yet the most damage happens there. Tim's cones are able to withstand the high winds of a tornado. When the high winds hit, pressure is spread out along the perimeter of the cone, causing it to stick to the ground like a suction cup. Dropping a probe with precision in front of a tornado takes real skill. The Argonauts practiced this technique as a hypothetical tornado barreled straight at them.

Photo by Jude Kesl

Scientists continue to explore these weather events. From the collected data, they design laboratory experiments and computer models to better understand monster weather. Yet, even with all this effort, it is not possible with today's science to predict precisely when or where a tornado will strike. That is why the work of Tim Samaras is so important. Perhaps his probes will record the elusive clues that will help unlock the answers to these questions. 🌀

What's in a Map?

Tim Samaras uses radar and satellite images and shared weather databases, as well as instant communication with other storm chasers and scientists, to track severe thunderstorms and tornadoes. As Tim assimilates this data, he is able to predict where tornadoes may form. The use of a simple weather map provides Tim with vital clues to the movement of a storm system across a region.

Understanding weather maps and making predictions are vitally important. People depend on weather news to grow their crops, conduct business, and plan leisure activities. In this lab, you will interpret a weather map and develop your own prediction.

Weather Forecast for Friday, March 09, 2007
DOC/NOAA/NWS/NCEP/Hydrometeorological Prediction Center
Prepared by Otto based on HPC, SPC, and TFC forecasts.

National Oceanic and Atmospheric Administration (NOAA)

Materials
- **Lab 4 Data Sheet**
- **weather map**
- **paper and pencil**
- **Internet access**

Lab Prep

Practice interpreting a weather map. Refer to the key on the next page and the "Common Weather Symbols and their Meanings" chart on the inside back cover of this book. Use these questions to guide you.

1. Look at the map on page 63. Does it make sense that New Mexico and Colorado are experiencing tornadoes? Why?

2. The weather map shows high and low pressure centers across the United States. Research wind direction around pressure centers and draw indicators to show your best estimate of air flow around these pressure centers. Note the **isobars** indicating areas of equal pressure measurements around each pressure center.

3. Write a brief, current weather report for regions of the United States (Northeast, South, Midwest, Central Plains, Rockies, West, and Northwest) based on your interpretation of the symbols on this weather map.

4. Based on your interpretation of the weather map, write a brief weather forecast for the next 24 hours for the same regions of the United States (Northeast, South, Midwest, Central Plains, Rockies, West and Northwest).

5. Do you see a link between weather events and weather **fronts**? Look at other weather maps and discuss your observations with your teacher.

Make Observations

1. Go to *http://www.noaa.gov* and type your zip code into the "Local Forecast" search box. The page you now see has your "Current Conditions" in the right-hand column. Record the weather data in your area.

2. From your browser, click the Back button, and the national "Warnings and Forecasts" map will appear. Click on the map as close to your city as you can, and a regional map will appear. Click on at least four other cities from this regional map, and find and record their local current weather conditions.

3. Using either a map from the NOAA website or your own drawing, plot the current conditions of each town using the appropriate weather symbols. Is the weather the same at each location? Why do you think this is so?

4. Using the current conditions, predict how the weather will change in your town and in the other towns you researched over the next 8 hours. Be specific about wind speed, direction, and dew point. Record your predictions.

5. Before you go to bed tonight, go back to the NOAA website and look at the current conditions for each town. Were your predictions correct? Why or why not?

6. Using this data as evidence, how do you think the weather in your town will change in the next 24 hours?

Weather Map

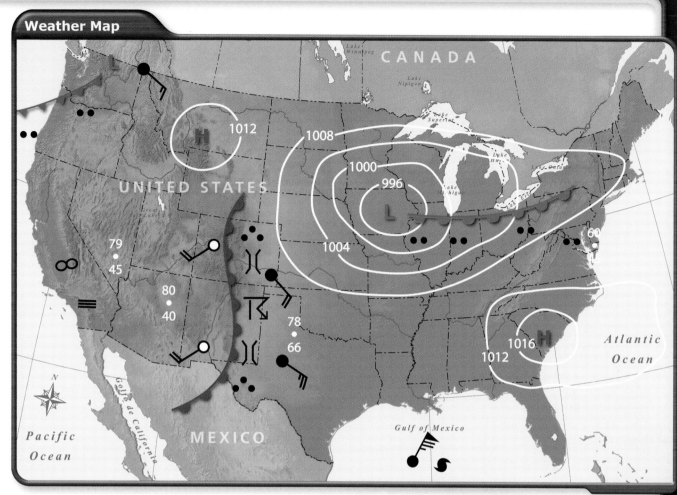

7. Why do you think it is important to use more than one town's data for predictions?

8. By using the data you collected, could you predict weather conditions in the other towns you looked at?

Extension

Determine four locations at least 200 miles away from you in various directions. Select locations that would be good predictors of the weather you are likely to experience in the near future. Then go back to the NOAA website to gather weather data at these four locations. Click on the "2 Day History" link below "Current Conditions" for each of these locations and note the recent weather there. Describe your weather in the next 24 hours, and explain why you chose these particular locations as predictors.

 Journal Question How do you think people were affected by much less accurate weather predictions before the tools we use today were invented?

Weather Map Key

L = Low Pressure Air pressure measured in millibars	**H** = High Pressure Air pressure measured in millibars	= Warm Front
= Cold Front	= Stationary Front	= Dry Line
⊤5 = Thunderstorms		**S** = Hurricane
⌇⌇ = Smoke		)(= Tornado or Funnel Cloud
∞ = Haze		≡ = Heavy Fog
⌒⌇ = Freezing Rain		•• = Rain

Station Model Symbols

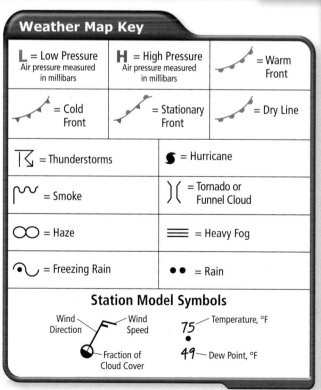

Wind Direction — Wind Speed — Temperature, °F 75
•
Fraction of Cloud Cover — 49 — Dew Point, °F

Predicting Severe Weather

Recall that your mission is to **alert your community to the threat of thunderstorms and tornadoes by tracking elusive clues in the atmosphere.** Now that you have been fully briefed, it is time to complete your mission and alert your community to the threat of a severe storm.

When Tim Samaras looks for severe weather, he analyzes many types of data in order to identify the location of the dry line. Then, he and his team race toward the storm. You will analyze the weather data you collect and determine, just as Tim does, whether a storm will develop in your community.

Mission 3 Argonaut Field Assignment Video Join the National Argonauts as they chase storms with Tim Samaras. See how they prepare to go into the field, collect critical weather data, and predict a storm in Denver, Colorado.

Objectives: To complete your mission, accomplish the following:

- Design and document a procedure to collect weather intelligence.
- Enter your weather intelligence in a data collection chart online or on paper.
- Develop a weather forecast for severe storms over the next two days for your community.
- Report your forecast to your school community.

Materials

- **Mission 3 Field Assignment Data Sheet**
- **barometer** (p. 112)
- **wind vane** (p. 112)
- **anemometer** (p. 113)
- **dew point tool** (p. 114)
- **paper and pencil**
- **cloud chart**
- **digital camera** (optional)

Map 1: Air Temperature and Dew Point

This map shows air temperature (upper number) and dew point temperature (lower number) in degrees Fahrenheit for several locations in Tornado Alley.

Field Preparation

Analyze Map 1 as directed and answer the questions below.

1. Use the dew point data to locate the dry line. Draw the dry line on your copy of Map 1.

2. Shade the side of the dry line on which severe weather is *most likely* to develop.

3. Explain how you chose the area where severe weather is *most likely* to develop.

4. Why is severe weather *most likely* to develop close to the dry line?

5. What is the significance of the dew point on the map?

Now study Map 2 on the next page and answer the following questions.

6. In which direction is the wind blowing in the area that has the highest risk of severe weather?

⑦ Are air masses converging? Explain your reasoning.

⑧ List the most important factors to consider when determining the likelihood of severe weather. Why did you choose those factors?

Mission Challenge

Using the tools you have built to gather weather data, design a procedure for collecting data near your home. Use the data to help you forecast whether severe weather will occur within the next 24 hours. Also be sure to use the cloud chart to help you identify the clouds you see. Go to the **JASON Mission Center** to download this resource. Use the questions below to help you make some decisions.

① What information do you need to collect?

② When and where will you gather data?

③ How many times do you need to collect data?

④ If you have access to a digital camera, take photos of the cloud cover you observe every time you collect data.

After you have developed your procedure, perform your data collection. Be sure to record your procedure, materials, and all measurements you take. Write a forecast based on your collected data. Will it storm overnight? In the morning? Later tomorrow afternoon? Not at all? Report your forecast to others in your household. Be sure to have an adult sign your forecast so that your teacher will know that you've completed your work!

Back at mission control (your classroom), post your data on the map your teacher provides. Be sure to use the weather symbols you've learned so far!

Mission Debrief

Now that you have completed the action part of the mission, let us see whether you have obtained the knowledge that you need to accomplish your goal.

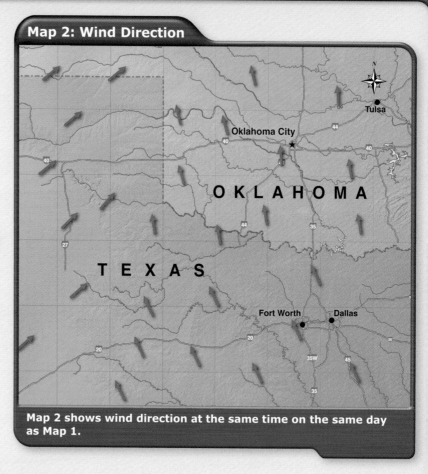

Map 2: Wind Direction

Map 2 shows wind direction at the same time on the same day as Map 1.

① Was your local weather forecast accurate? Why or why not?

② What information would have helped you make a more accurate forecast?

③ How did the clouds you observed (or the lack of clouds) affect your forecast? Use photos, if you have them, to support your forecast.

④ If energy is associated with heat, light, and electricity, explain how energy is moved around in Earth's atmosphere through weather events.

⑤ Storms are a natural part of Earth's processes, but sometimes they are harmful to people and cause damage to the environment. How are storms *helpful* to people and the environment?

 Journal Question What should people think about before they build homes and businesses or plan activities in places where monster storms are common? Explain your answers.

GRAPHING
Tornadic Air Pressure

An F4 tornado has touched down. As it rips a path across the land, Tim Samaras races to position his probes. Known as "turtles," these instrument packs are built to collect data during extreme weather conditions and survive the encounter. With luck, this tornado will continue on the course Tim has predicted, and will pass close to at least one of the probes.

On this day, however, the incredible has happened. The raging twister crosses directly over one of the instrument packs! It is the first time the innermost structure of a tornado is revealed and recorded.

Obtaining this type of data is only the first step in understanding a weather event. Next, you need to organize and analyze the information. From this analysis, you can better understand the structure and behavior of the tornado. And once the analysis is complete, you need to communicate your findings to others. This is where graphs come in. Graphs are used to display, organize, and communicate information.

Your Turn

Suppose you collected data on two tornadoes. How might graphs of your measurements help you compare and contrast these two twisters? Well, here is your chance to find out. The tables on this page display the data collected on two tornadoes. Let us assume that each twister crossed directly over a probe. Follow the steps to analyze and compare these tornadoes.

Tornado A

Time (seconds)	Pressure (millibars)
0	960
20	965
40	950
60	955
80	900
100	880
120	880
140	905
160	950
180	960

Tornado B

Time (seconds)	Pressure (millibars)
0	980
20	980
40	970
60	980
80	965
100	850
120	930
140	970
160	965
180	970

Steps

1. Create a line graph of each data set. Place Time on the horizontal axis and Pressure on the vertical axis.

2. What is your independent variable and what is your dependent variable? Explain.

3. How many minutes of data are displayed?

4. Identify the lowest pressure and the time it was recorded for each tornado.

5. Slope is a ratio, or rate. In this model, what does the slope of each line segment indicate? What is the graph doing when slope is negative? What is happening to air pressure? What is the graph doing when slope is positive? What is happening to air pressure?

6. What does a steeper slope in a graph mean? Which twister showed the most rapid change in air pressure, and in what timeframe did it occur?

7. If both twisters moved at the same speed, which twister had the larger low-pressure region? How can you tell?

Air pressure is measured in units called millibars (mb). At sea level on Earth's surface, the standard pressure averages about 1013 mb. Although this seems like a big number, do not expect it to vary much. In most places, the air pressure ranges between 970 mb and 1030 mb. And when it drops out of that range, watch out! Monster weather may be on the way.

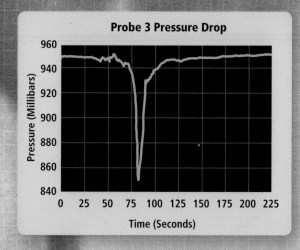

Probe 3 Pressure Drop

Working with Real Data

Imagine stepping into an elevator and rising 100 stories skyward in just ten seconds! That is the way Tim described the change in air pressure measured in his F4 tornado. Here is a graph showing that very data. Can you interpret it?

1. What was the atmospheric pressure before and after the tornado appeared?

2. What was the lowest pressure recorded and when was it observed?

3. Compare and contrast all three tornadoes using Tim's graph with the two graphs you constructed.

The Hunt
Flying into the Eye

"With all of the data we're collecting, we know that we can improve hurricane forecasting and tracking. For the people in the path of a hurricane, we're hoping that we can make a difference."

—Jason Dunion
Research Meteorologist, NOAA

UNITED STATES DEP'T OF COMMERCE

Jason Dunion

Jason Dunion and other NOAA scientists use aircraft such as the P-3 turboprop to collect data about hurricanes.

 Meet the Researchers Video
Learn about Jason's research on hot, dry, and dusty air that stops hurricanes in their tracks.

Research Meteorologist, NOAA

 **Read more about Jason Dunion
online in the JASON Mission Center.**

Your Mission...

Predict a hurricane's track and intensity by studying its source of energy, its formation, and its decay.

To accomplish your mission successfully, you will need to

- Understand the structure and dynamic nature of a hurricane.
- Explain what fuels a hurricane.
- Describe the conditions necessary for a hurricane to form.
- Investigate the weakening and decay of hurricanes.
- Explore how scientists study and track hurricanes.

Join the Team

In Miami, Host Researcher Jason Dunion briefs the Argonauts on the technological advances used to monitor hurricanes, and on his current research on the Saharan Air Layer. This air layer event suppresses hurricane formation in the Atlantic Ocean. Satellites can observe this hot, dry, and dusty air at specific electromagnetic radiation frequencies that are not visible to the human eye. In addition, Jason uses airplanes called hurricane hunters that are specially modified for the extreme environment of a hurricane. These planes fly right through storms and into the eye of a hurricane to measure atmospheric conditions. The data they gather help researchers predict when and where storms will occur and how they will behave. From left: Teacher Argonaut Christine Sills Arnold, Student Argonaut Matthew Worsham, Host Researcher Jason Dunion, Student Argonauts Lauren Groskaufmanis and Cassandra Santamaria.

Photo by Peter Haydock, The JASON Project

Flying into the Eye

A powerful hurricane is moving toward the East Coast of the United States. While most people are trying to flee the path of the storm, a group of scientists is flying directly into it! The flight is a roller coaster ride. Violent winds toss the plane like a Frisbee™, slamming it down toward the ocean and then flinging it skyward. One of the scientists onboard is Jason Dunion, a research meteorologist with NOAA's Hurricane Research Division. Working with NOAA, Jason has flown many hurricane-hunter missions like this one.

Hurricane-hunter flights are a dramatic way of learning about hurricanes. The flights typically last about ten hours, during which time the airplane crosses the storm many times. The information collected provides a detailed picture of the storm's structure and conditions, including wind speed and direction, atmospheric pressure, temperature, and precipitation. This data is fed into computer programs that predict the hurricane's path and strength.

As a scientist, Jason Dunion is trying to solve the problems of understanding hurricanes. One of the most intriguing problems is why some strong hurricanes suddenly and unpredictably lose strength in spite of what the computer models forecast. Jason thinks that the answer may lie in a layer of hot, dry, and dusty air.

Strap in for a mission that will have you exploring the dynamics of hurricanes. With the Argonaut team, you will investigate how hurricanes form, intensify, and decay.

 Mission 4 Briefing Video See how Jason uses his knowledge of hurricane development to predict the strength and track of a hurricane.

▼ Tropical cyclones, which include hurricanes, typhoons, and cyclones, have a complex structure of clouds, rain, and winds. This illustration shows the counterclockwise rotation of a storm in the Northern Hemisphere.

Warm, moist air spirals upward in the eyewall. As the air spirals out of the top of the hurricane, it spreads ice crystals over the storm. These ice crystals form a layer of cirrus clouds that covers the hurricane. The highest winds and heaviest rain occur in the eyewall.

The eye is the center of a hurricane. Air sinks slowly in the eye. The eye usually has calm weather.

Mission Briefing
Tropical Cyclones

Hurricanes are a type of **tropical cyclone.** Tropical cyclones are massive tropical storms with extremely strong winds that spiral around a center of low air pressure. These storms form over warm ocean waters around the world. Because warm water fuels them, they typically form in tropical waters within 5 to 25 degrees latitude north or south of the equator. Prevailing winds can then steer them to latitudes farther north or south of the equator. Tropical cyclones are variously named in different parts of the world. Those that form in the western Pacific Ocean are called **typhoons.** Those that form in the Indian Ocean and the South Pacific Ocean are called **cyclones.** Those that form in the Atlantic Ocean and eastern Pacific are called **hurricanes.**

In the Northern Hemisphere tropical cyclones spiral counterclockwise, whereas in the Southern Hemisphere they spiral in a clockwise direction. The spiraling of the winds is produced by Earth's rotation. The phenomenon is known as the **Coriolis Effect.** Generally, the farther from the equator a storm is positioned, the more this phenomenon affects the storm.

A hurricane typically has a circular shape and an average diameter of about 480 km (300 mi). The storms are made up of many bands of thunderstorms that spiral outward in a counterclockwise direction from a central "eye."

The **eye** of the hurricane is a circular region with few clouds and very light winds at the center of the storm. This is the calmest part of the storm. Not every hurricane has an eye; but, if one develops, its diameter usually ranges from about 8 km (5 mi) to over 200 km (120 mi). A hurricane's eye has the lowest surface air pressure in the storm. Scientists measure the air pressure in the eye to understand and forecast how strong the storm will be. Air in the center of the eye slowly sinks from above, becoming warmer and drier as it sinks. For this reason, a hurricane's eye has few clouds.

The region surrounding a hurricane's eye is called the **eyewall.** The eyewall is a wall of clouds and is usually considered the most deadly part of the hurricane. Moist air rises through the spiraling winds of the eyewall, releasing heat as an energy source for the hurricane. As the air rises, water vapor condenses and tall thunderstorms form. Heavy rain and extreme wind characterize the eyewall.

Many **rainbands** exist beyond the eyewall. Rainbands are regions of heavy thunderstorms that spiral outward from the center of the hurricane. The strongest rainbands usually occur 90 degrees clockwise to the track of the storm. The thunderstorms form where moist air rises. Areas of lighter precipitation separate the rainbands. In these areas, air does not rise as much or may even sink.

Rainbands form where moist air rises. They have a spiral shape around the center of the hurricane.

In the Northern Hemisphere, strong winds blow around the hurricane in a counterclockwise direction.

Illustration by Greg Harris

Lockheed WP-3D Orion "Hurricane Hunter"

The aircraft collects weather data using onboard radar and by launching data-transmitting probes called dropsondes. Once dropped from the plane, the instruments in these probes collect data on altitude, horizontal wind speed, air temperature, and humidity. The dropsondes radio the data back to the hurricane hunter plane as they descend by parachute through the storm.

Length: 35.6 m (116 ft 10 in.)

Wingspan: 30.4 m (99 ft 8 in.)

Empty mass (weight): 27,900 kg (61,500 lb)

Maximum mass (weight): 63,400 kg (139,771 lb)

Power plant: 4 turboprop engines

Maximum speed: 745 km/h (466 mph)

Maximum working altitude: 7600 m (25,000 ft)

Range at low altitude: 4120 km (2560 mi); at high altitude: 6100 km (3800 mi)

Crew: up to 18 (9 flight crew and 9 researchers or observers)

Onboard data collection: The planes collect flight-level wind speed, direction, and humidity. In addition to these measurements, two radar instruments collect data on the storm and are located beneath the plane and in the tail. The tail radar is a Doppler unit and collects the best data on the storm, but does not record the forward radar images. The radar on the belly of the plane is a standard weather radar instrument and collects weather data all around the plane. Scientists can build a complete 3-D picture of the storm using these two sets of radar. A third radar in the nose of the plane is for flight navigation only and is not part of the weather instrumentation.

- Although more than 700 Orion aircraft have been manufactured, only two have been outfitted as hurricane hunters.
- The Orion hurricane hunters are nicknamed Kermit and Miss Piggy. NOAA's third hurricane hunter is a smaller Gulfstream IV aircraft called Gonzo.
- The Orion hurricane hunters are not specially reinforced to withstand hurricane winds.
- In addition to NOAA's three aircraft, the Air Force Reserve Command uses ten WC-130 Hercules aircraft as hurricane hunters.

How Hurricanes Form

The energy source that a hurricane needs in order to form and strengthen is warm ocean water. As ocean water evaporates and forms water vapor, heat energy is carried up into the atmosphere. Then, when the water vapor condenses back into liquid water in a cloud, it releases this stored heat energy. The rising air spirals and produces a low-pressure zone at the surface where thunderstorms begin to form. As these thunderstorms become more organized, they produce a cluster called a tropical disturbance. Under certain conditions, this storm system can continue to strengthen and begin to rotate, leading to the formation of a hurricane. These conditions include

- sea-surface temperatures that are typically warmer than about 27°C (80°F).
- the exchange of heat energy from the ocean up into the atmosphere.
- light winds outside the system that create convections but are not strong enough to topple the buildup of the hurricane's tall clouds, or that do not tear apart the rotational motion in the developing storm.

If one or more of these conditions does not exist, a hurricane will not form, or an existing hurricane will decay.

Why Hurricanes Weaken

A hurricane may weaken or decay for several reasons. These reasons include high wind shear; moving over cooler ocean water; having its moist, rising air stopped or dried out; and moving over land. Let us consider each of these reasons in turn.

Suppose you are measuring wind speed and direction close to the ground. Then suppose you could continue taking measurements on a ladder rising straight up into the atmosphere. If the wind speed or direction changes as you climb, you are measuring wind shear. **Wind shear** is a change in wind speed and/or direction at different heights in the atmosphere. The amount of wind shear is critical to the development or destruction of a hurricane. Hurricanes need some wind shear to form storm convections and intensify, but too much shear can rip the storm apart.

Low wind shear allows a hurricane to form and grow stronger. Warm, moist air can rise to form clouds and convection can develop. High wind shear can tear a hurricane apart. Surface winds may move the lower part of a hurricane in one direction while higher-level winds blow the top part in a different direction.

Hurricanes also weaken when they move over cooler water. Cool ocean water does not evaporate as much as warm ocean water does. Less evaporation means that less energy is transferred from the ocean to the atmosphere. With less energy, a hurricane weakens or decays.

Wind Shear in Hurricanes

Wind shear is important to hurricane development. Jason Dunion and his colleagues look for light wind shear to help foster the growth of a monster storm. Without wind shear a convection cell does not form, but too much wind shear can tear the storm apart.

You have probably experienced wind shear. If you have ever been in a car that was passed by a large semitrailer truck on the highway, you might recall your car being rocked back and forth as the truck passed. That "disturbance" is the result of wind shear. Now imagine what even stronger wind shear can do to a hurricane.

In this lab, you will build a model to examine the effects of wind shear on the updrafts that fuel a monster storm.

Materials
- Lab 1 Data Sheet
- several blocks or books
- 1 box fan or window fan
- multiple Mylar™ streamers
- tape
- protractor
- 2 hair dryers with low and high speeds

Lab Prep

1. Begin to assemble the model by placing the blocks or books on the floor in an arrangement that will support the fan as it lays on top. Stack the supports to a height of at least 10 cm (4 in.). Lay the fan on its back on top of the blocks so that it is blowing upward. Use tape to attach several Mylar™ streamers (each approximately 1 m long) to the front of the fan. Position them around the inner area of the fan grating, about one-third the distance from its center to its outer edge. What do you expect the streamers to do when you turn the fan on? What do they represent in this model?

2. Plug in the fan and turn it on. What do the streamers actually do?

3. What does the fan represent in this model?

Make Observations

Using the model built in the Lab Prep section above, demonstrate how wind shear can impact convection in a hurricane. Design an experiment using hair dryer position, height, and speed to produce varying amounts of wind shear, and answer the following questions.

Record your data for each case, and describe the effects you observe. Include the height of each hair dryer and hair dryer settings. Looking at your model from above, use the protractor to estimate and record the angle between the directions of the two hair dryers.

1. From the data that you collect, identify the level of wind shear and conditions that prove that you have stopped the hurricane. What evidence in the model leads you to this conclusion?

2. From the data that you collect, identify the level of wind shear and conditions that can move a hurricane and still maintain the convections. What evidence in the model leads you to this conclusion?

 Journal Question Describe the decay of a hurricane, using what you have learned from your reading and your experiments.

Team Highlight
MATTHEW WORSHAM
Student Argonaut, Ohio

Student Argonaut Matthew Worsham tries on an official P-3 Hurricane Hunter flight suit like the one researcher Jason Dunion wears. The suit is designed to keep the wearer warm, and, as Matthew discovered, it has plenty of pockets to keep things in. P-3 Hurricane Hunters also carry fireproof survival suits, just in case the crew members have to bail out of the plane.

Photo by Peter Haydock, The JASON Project

Evolution of a Hurricane

Normally, several hurricanes form in the Atlantic Ocean each year between June and November—what we call hurricane season. Some of these hurricanes affect the United States. Follow the stages to learn how these hurricanes form.

Stage 5: Landfall
When a hurricane moves ashore, it brings violent winds, heavy rains, and high ocean waves. Then as it moves over land, the storm is no longer able to feed on the energy it gets from the warm ocean, and it starts to slowly dissipate.

Stage 4: A Hurricane Forms
As air pressure in a tropical storm continues to drop, winds intensify. When the wind speed reaches 119 km/h (74 mph), a tropical storm becomes a hurricane. The structure of a hurricane is highly organized, and winds rotate around an eye which will typically form at its center.

Stage 3: The Tropical Depression Becomes a Tropical Storm
When wind speeds in a tropical depression reach 63 km/h (39 mph), the system becomes a tropical storm. At this time, the storm is given a name following an alphabetical assignment each year. The structure and rotation of named tropical storms are better-defined than are those of a tropical depression.

Fast Fact

The highest sea-surface temperatures on Earth have been measured in the tropics of the western Pacific Ocean. Average summer sea-surface temperature in this region is near 30°C (86°F). These high temperatures and the large area of ocean waters, where storms can intensify, allow some of the strongest storms on Earth to form. The region also has an average of about 16 typhoons each year. By comparison, the Atlantic Ocean averages only about six hurricanes each year.

Where Tropical Cyclones Form

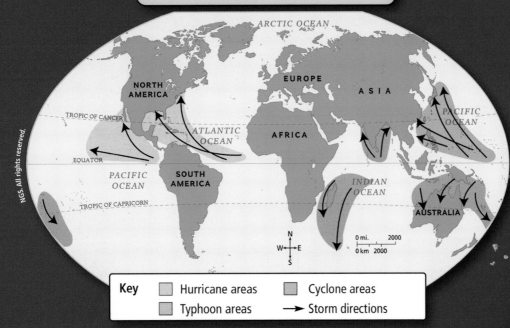

Key
- Hurricane areas
- Typhoon areas
- Cyclone areas
- → Storm directions

Hurricane-like storms form in many parts of the world, but they have different names in different places.

Stage 1: A Tropical Disturbance Forms

Most Atlantic hurricanes begin life as organized clusters of thunderstorms off the west coast of Africa. These thunderstorms form along waves in the prevailing trade winds. The waves, called easterly waves, can be more than 2500 km (1550 mi) long. The cluster of thunderstorms is called a tropical disturbance.

Stage 2: The Tropical Disturbance Becomes a Tropical Depression

Most tropical disturbances die out, but some can continue to grow if they cross warm ocean water. Rising, warm air lowers the pressure and causes surface winds to rush in. The moisture carried aloft releases heat energy when it condenses. This causes more air to rise and surface winds to intensify further in a chain reaction that strengthens the storm. The system, which has now become a tropical depression, contains a distinct surface wind circulation with winds as high as 61 km/h (38 mph) and has started to rotate in a counterclockwise direction due to Earth's spin.

Scientific Visualization Studio/NASA Goddard Space Flight Center

Interpreting Hurricane Data

Scientists like Jason Dunion rely on satellite images like the one you see on the next page to help them determine whether a hurricane will develop, where it might strike, and how much damage it might cause. Scientists combine this data with additional data from land and airborne sources to form a more accurate forecast that can help save lives and property in the path of the storm. Scientists can also help clarify which communities do and do not need to evacuate. This allows for easier and safer movement of people who do need to evacuate, and helps communities save money when managing the storm event.

The image on the next page shows Hurricane Rita just before it made landfall in September 2005. In this lab, you will analyze the image to see what data it can yield.

Materials
- **Lab 2 Data Sheet**
- **Hurricane Rita satellite image** (p. 77)
- **ruler**

Lab Prep

1. How are clouds, water, and land represented in the satellite image?

2. What region of the United States is visible in the image?

3. Which states are outlined on the map?

4. What is happening in the whitest areas of the image? Explain.

5. What is happening in the areas where there are few or no clouds?

Team Highlight

JEANNETTE D. WILLIAMS-SMITH
Argonaut Alumnus, Florida

Host Researcher Jason Dunion (right) chats with Jeannette D. Williams-Smith while checking out the P-3 Hurricane Hunter aircraft.

Photo by Peter Haydock, The JASON Project

Make Observations

1. How far onto land do the rainbands reach? Use the scale on the image to determine the distance.

2. What is the overall size of the storm (in kilometers and in miles)?

3. In which direction is Hurricane Rita rotating? How do you know?

4. Where is the strongest part of the storm in this image? How do you know?

5. In which direction is Hurricane Rita moving?

6. How will Hurricane Rita change after it makes landfall? How do you know?

7. What are the advantages to using satellite images to learn about hurricanes? What are some disadvantages?

8. What other images would be helpful in determining Rita's intensity and track? Explain your answer.

Journal Question What would you tell people who live along the coast (or inland) where Rita is approaching? What do you think cities should do before the storm to help protect their citizens?

Digital Lab Join Jason Dunion in predicting the intensity and track of hurricanes in the Digital Lab *Storm Tracker*. Issue hurricane warnings to notify communities of the impending danger of the storm. Compete against other storm trackers around the world to see who is the best storm tracker!

This image from NASA's Aqua satellite shows Hurricane Rita just before making landfall in September 2005.

Scale

0	50	100 miles

0	50	100	150 km

Jeff Schmaltz, MODIS Rapid Response Team, NASA/GSFC

A hurricane can move over cool water in several ways. Prevailing winds can steer a hurricane away from the band of warm tropical waters where it forms. This happens frequently along the Atlantic coast of the United States. A hurricane also could move into an area where a cold ocean current flows. The cold ocean current off the coast of California helps prevent Pacific typhoons from reaching that state's coastline. Finally, a hurricane may pass over cold water that was stirred up by an earlier storm. The stirred water is cooler because cool water from beneath the surface mixes with the warm water near the surface.

Jason Dunion recently discovered that another atmospheric event seems to impact hurricane development. His analysis of old satellite images shows that a layer of hot, dry, and dusty air from Africa might prevent or weaken some Atlantic Ocean hurricanes. His current research is to determine whether such an air mass can truly suppress hurricane development. Jason is using NOAA's hurricane hunter airplanes to study this more closely.

▲ This satellite picture shows a storm over North Africa pushing dry, dust-laden air—the Saharan Air Layer—out over the Atlantic.

Fast Fact

The Saharan Air Layer carries dust from Africa long distances. African dust forms a layer of red mud at the bottom of large parts of the Atlantic Ocean. It can also blow all the way to the southeast coast of the United States.

This air mass, called the **Saharan Air Layer,** forms over North Africa during the summer. At times, the Saharan air blows out over the moist air layer that is just above the water of the Atlantic Ocean. When it moves westward over the Atlantic, the Saharan Air Layer interrupts the updrafts that help strengthen a hurricane.

For the most part, temperatures in the atmosphere decrease with height. The Saharan Air Layer, however, causes a temperature inversion when it spreads over the Atlantic Ocean. When a **temperature inversion** occurs, a layer of warmer, less dense air lies above a layer of relatively cooler, more dense air. With this layered structure, air that has been warmed by the sun stays near the ocean's surface, and the water vapor made through evaporation cannot rise through the "cap" of the warmer, less dense Saharan air. If moist surface air cannot rise to higher altitudes, energy is not carried up into the atmosphere; towering storm clouds cannot develop; and a hurricane cannot form.

An encounter with the Saharan Air Layer can also affect a hurricane in other ways. If a hurricane approaches such an air layer, some of the dry air can mix into the storm. This robs the storm of moisture and decreases the transfer of heat energy to the atmosphere. Yet another way that the Saharan Air Layer can weaken a hurricane is by wind shear. High wind speeds in a Saharan Air Layer can produce strong wind shear that can tear a hurricane apart.

Landfall can also weaken a hurricane rapidly by robbing it of moisture and heat when it comes ashore. When a hurricane makes landfall, its source of energy—warm ocean water—is cut off. The storm quickly begins to decay. Its winds slow, and its structure becomes less organized. Although weakened, it can still cause damage. High winds may persist for a couple of days. Heavy rains may fall far inland. The hurricane can affect weather patterns over a large region, even as it travels over land and becomes a less severe storm.

Saharan Air Layer

Could dust from the Sahara Desert have anything to do with hurricanes? Jason Dunion is trying to determine whether hot, dry, dusty air could influence the formation and the strength of Atlantic hurricanes. Check out the satellite image on page 78 to see what such an air mass looks like.

In this activity, you will build a model to investigate the Saharan Air Layer phenomenon.

Materials

- Lab 3 Data Sheet
- large clear container
- medium container
- small plastic cup
- weights (large metal nut)
- food coloring (red and blue)
- kitchen plastic wrap
- rubber band
- scissors
- wax pencil
- pencil with a sharp point
- ice water
- warm water
- room temperature water
- safety goggles
- thermometer

Lab Prep

1. Put on your safety goggles. Place a large metal nut in the small cup to act as a weight. Add a few drops of blue food coloring and then fill the cup to its brim with room temperature water. Take the temperature of the water in the cup and record the data.

2. Make sure the blue coloring in the cup is mixed thoroughly, and then cover the cup with a piece of kitchen plastic wrap. Pull it tight over the top of the cup, and secure it with a rubber band to ensure a tight seal.

3. Position the sealed cup in the center of the large plastic container. Slowly fill the large clear plastic container with ice water at least 3 cm above the top of the small cup. Remove any pieces of ice that might have transferred into the container. Take the temperature of the ice water and record the data.

4. With a very sharp pencil, poke several small holes in the plastic wrap covering the small cup. Observe and describe what happens as the colored water mixes with the cold water in the larger container.

Next, you will build a new model to observe a temperature inversion layer similar to that present in a Saharan Air Layer event.

5. Clean out both the large container and the small cup. Repeat steps 1 through 3 to set up the experiment again. Be sure to take the temperature of the water in the small cup and the ice water, and record those values again.

6. Use a wax pencil to mark the height of the ice-chilled water on the outside of the large container.

7. Place a sheet of plastic wrap on the surface of the ice-chilled water so that it goes edge to edge inside the container, like a blanket that covers the water below.

8. In the medium-sized container, add warm water, enough to fill another 3–5 cm (about 1–2 in.) in the large container, and add red food coloring. Take the temperature of the warm water and record the data. Carefully pour the warm, red-colored water onto the surface of the plastic wrap inside the large container.

9. Gently remove the plastic wrap barrier.

10. Once again, use a sharp pencil to gently poke holes in the plastic wrap that is sealing the small cup in the bottom of the large container. Do not cause any stirring motion as you do this.

Make Observations

1. Describe what happens when you poke holes into the plastic wrap on the small cup.

2. For several minutes, carefully observe the movement of the dyed water that emerges from the cup. What path does it follow? Describe the movement that you observe. Why do you think this is happening?

Interpret Data

1. Explain the relationship between the temperatures of the three water samples and the mixing behavior that you observed.

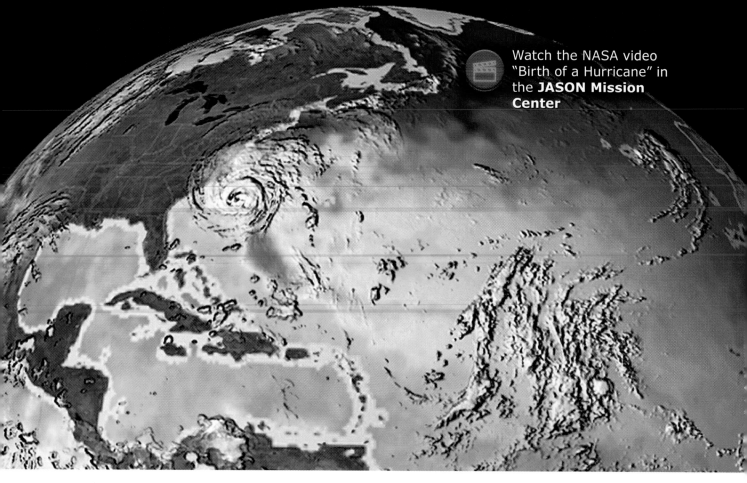

Watch the NASA video "Birth of a Hurricane" in the **JASON Mission Center**

▲ This satellite image shows how cold ocean water (in dark blue) is drawn to the surface in the wake of Hurricane Fabian, positioned off the Carolina coast.

Tracking Hurricanes

When hurricanes are far from land, satellites are the best way to gather information about them. Hurricane hunter aircraft can also fly through an approaching storm to collect firsthand observations. When a hurricane gets closer to land, ground-based Doppler radar and weather stations record valuable information.

Satellites are important data-gathering tools. They can show large portions of Earth's surface at one time and can also gather huge amounts of data very quickly. Specially equipped satellites detect parts of the electromagnetic spectrum that human eyes cannot see. This capability allows satellites to measure many different properties of hurricanes at the same time. Some satellite images show the locations of storms, sea-surface temperature, and wind speed and direction. Some satellite images are photographs taken with visible light. Infrared satellite images show temperature data. These images can be collected during the day or night.

Satellites are great for collecting large amounts of data over wide regions. But better yet, a hurricane hunter airplane can get data directly from within a hurricane. Researchers fly these specially equipped planes right through hurricanes to collect a variety of weather data. Another purpose for the flights is to determine the exact location of the hurricane's eye, which is difficult to track from a satellite. Jason Dunion participates in these flights so that he can gain a better understanding of hurricanes.

In addition to the battery of instruments located on the airplane, scientists also release probes called *dropsondes* into

NOAA Photo Library/NOAA in Space Collection

▲ GOES satellites provide weather data on a global scale.

Lockheed WP-3D Orion

Doppler radar instrument

Dropsonde instrument package launch chutes

Standard weather radar

NOAA flies two P-3 Hurricane Hunter aircraft. Their nicknames are Kermit and Miss Piggy.

the storm. A **dropsonde** is an instrument package designed to be dropped from an aircraft by a parachute. Many dropsondes are launched during a hurricane-hunter flight. When released from an airplane, the dropsonde descends on its parachute through the storm to the ocean below, taking a series of measurements as it falls. Sensors measure wind speed and direction, temperature, humidity, and air pressure. Its radio transmitter sends a stream of data, including its location, to a computer back onboard the airplane. In this way, the data collected by a dropsonde helps researchers produce a vertical profile of the features of a storm and build 3-D models of the event.

Ground-based instruments, including Doppler radar, also collect hurricane data. **Doppler radar** stations, positioned in a grid system that covers the continental United States, use radar to "see" through clouds, locate areas of precipitation, and estimate rates of precipitation. This radar also measures the motion of water droplets toward or away from the radar. Scientists use this information to calculate wind speed and direction within the storm. Doppler radar provides detailed data about a hurricane's wind, rain, and the direction of its path. Unfortunately, the range of a Doppler radar unit is only about 400 km (250 mi). Because these systems are land-based and not at sea, a hurricane must be close to land before a Doppler radar unit can collect data on it.

Hundreds of weather observatories across the United States collect local weather data, including temperature, wind speed and direction, and precipitation. The observatories are useful for tracking and monitoring a hurricane after it comes ashore.

Forecasters analyze the data collected by all of these instruments and feed it into computer models. These models use math to simulate weather conditions in the atmosphere and help predict how hurricanes will move and change. Accuracy in predicting the probable path of a hurricane has improved dramatically, although predicting storm intensity remains difficult. The National Hurricane Center uses the computer model results and forecasters' analyses to issue hurricane watches and warnings.

▲ The instruments at automated surface weather stations provide a steady stream of weather data.

What's a Storm to Do?

Recall that your mission is to *predict a hurricane's track and intensity by studying its source of energy, its formation, and its decay.* Now that you have been fully briefed, it's time to make some observations using the same tools Jason Dunion uses to predict a hurricane's track and intensity. These tools include satellites, planes, and surface weather stations to determine whether a monster storm will form, where it will go, and what it will do. Using Jason's data and that of other scientists, NOAA helps cities and citizens prepare for these storms each year.

Objectives: To complete your mission, accomplish the following objectives:

- Analyze satellite images to determine whether a tropical storm will become a hurricane.
- Produce a proposal for a device or machine that influences hurricane development.
- Predict a storm's intensity and track.

Now that you know how storms form, what influences their strength, and how to interpret satellite images of storms, it's time to see what you can do! In this challenge, you will analyze satellite images of potential storms and then predict whether they will become monster storms. You will also write a proposal to NOAA for building a machine that can influence the development and behavior of these storms.

Materials
- **Mission 4 Field Assignment Data Sheet**
- **satellite images**
- **ruler**

Field Preparation

1. Look at the satellite image on the next page. How would you classify this storm (e.g., hurricane, tropical depression, tropical storm)?

2. What are the surrounding conditions that will influence the growth or decay of this storm?

3. Study the wind barbs in the image. In what direction is the storm moving?

4. Given the data from the satellite image, do you think the storm will strengthen or weaken? Why?

Mission Challenge

Using your knowledge of storm formation and what affects it, write a proposal to NOAA to obtain funding to build a machine that will either inhibit or enhance a storm's properties. Keep in mind that, while we may view hurricanes as largely destructive to humans, hurricanes are important natural events in other ecological life cycles. Many ecosystems rely on the rain that these storms bring; some ecosystems need the strong winds to blow down old and dead trees; and even the storm surges are part of a process that rebuilds coastal wetlands. Hurricane Katrina pushed an estimated 144 million tons of new sediment into the wetlands of Louisiana that will help rebuild barrier islands in the future.

Your proposal to NOAA should have the following components:

1. Brief overview (1–2 paragraphs) of what your machine will do.

2. Detailed description of how your machine will work, including the following:

   a. How it will influence the storm (what mechanisms it will use: the Saharan Air Layer, wind shear, temperature inversions, etc.).

   b. When you will deploy it (early in the storm formation process, just before it hits land, etc.).

3. Scientific evidence that the machine will work.

4. The advantages of using your machine, including:

   a. How will people, plants, animals, and the land benefit from your machine? What other positive outcomes will occur?

   b. What things will your machine prevent from being destroyed? What new things will be created by your machine?

5 The disadvantages of using your machine, including:

   a. How much rainfall different areas will receive.

   b. How it will affect ocean currents or ocean temperatures.

   c. Impact on animals and plants that live in the ocean.

Mission Debrief

1 Having studied satellite images throughout this mission, explain how these images would be useful to forecasters.

2 Why is understanding the formation of storms important to scientists?

3 Considering that these storms have lots of clouds (and therefore lots of water), how do they affect the weather of the areas where they reach land?

4 What might be the effect on the formation of hurricanes if ocean temperatures were to drop worldwide? What if ocean temperatures were to rise worldwide?

 Log onto the **JASON Mission Center** and predict a hurricane's track and intensity in the Digital Lab *Storm Tracker*.

 Journal Question Do you think that scientists should try to influence the formation, track, or intensity of hurricanes? Explain your answer.

100–250 MB
251–350 MB
351–500 MB

GOES-8 MID-UPPER LEVEL WINDS   1800 UTC   26OCT98   UW-CIMSS/NESDIS

Where in the World?

The Sahara is unlike any other place on our planet. It is the hot desert that is as large as an entire continent! The Sahara's varied landscape occupies the northern half of Africa, slicing this continent into the dry north, and the more lush, sub-Saharan region.

Petroglyphs

For nearly 3.5 million years, ancestral hominids have lived at the edge of this great desert. Over time, various cultures left their mark on its changing landscape. In the Air Mountains of the Sahara, stone age artists carved images in rock. Known as petroglyphs, the largest of these creations is a giraffe that is over 6 m (20 ft) long and was carved nearly 10,000 years ago!

Fossils

Imagine a crocodile as large as a school bus! It may seem like science fiction, but about 100 million years ago it was science fact. Scientists believe that these fierce and active predators devoured small dinosaurs in a single bite!

The remains of these giant crocodiles were uncovered in a fossil dig site. Like other deserts, the Sahara is a great place to unearth fossils. That is because the climate and the geologic history have worked together to preserve traces of prehistoric life.

A Changing Environment

The Saharan desert is a hot and dry place that formed several million years ago. However, thousands of years ago, parts of this great expanse of desert were a tropical grassland, supporting a diverse and rich ecosystem.

On the land, fossil evidence supports this theory of the Sahara's change. From space, ground-penetrating radar offers high-tech support for a more lush, ancient environment.

The upper image shows the sand covered landscape of the Safsaf Oasis in Egypt. The lower image illustrates the same region, but peers beneath the sandy surface with radar. Reflections from a deeper, buried rock landscape illustrate a river bed and a landform cut and shaped by flowing water.

Your Turn

Geography is much more than memorizing names and places on a map. It's really about formulating a knowledge of the world and all that's in it, on many levels and from many different perspectives. This includes Earth processes and patterns, landforms, cultures, resources, and the interactions of human populations with their environments. Research one aspect of Saharan geography that affects the world, and share what you learn as either a written report, poster session, or multimedia presentation to your classmates.

"I create a map based on the data I have collected. The map is given to hurricane forecasters and emergency managers to help improve their forecasting. Together we are saving property and lives."

—Shirley Murillo
Research Meteorologist, NOAA

Shirley Murillo

Shirley Murillo flies into hurricanes onboard one of NOAA's hurricane hunter airplanes. The planes are flying weather laboratories.

Meet the Researchers Video
Learn about Shirley's research on hurricane winds, and how what she learns can help save lives and minimize property damage.

Research Meteorologist, NOAA

Read more about Shirley online in the JASON Mission Center.

Your Mission...

Protect life and minimize the loss of vital assets before, during, and after a storm.

To accomplish your mission successfully, you will need to

- Understand the hazards of hurricanes.
- Explain the difference between hurricane watches and warnings.
- Study emergency planning and responses before, during, and after a hurricane.
- Investigate emergency planning and response for other weather events.
- Complete an action plan for emergency response before, during, and after a storm event.

Join the Team

Student Argonauts Cassandra Santamaria and Lauren Groskaufmanis, Teacher Argonaut Christine Sills Arnold, Host Researcher Shirley Murillo, and Student Argonaut Matthew Worsham study wind fields and discuss how hurricane winds impact cities like Miami, Florida. Understanding how winds tend to behave throughout the day at different locations is one thing that emergency response planners need to understand about monster weather. This information helps them develop response procedures to keep people out of harm's way and protect their property as well.

Photo by Peter Haydock, The JASON Project

Living with Monster Storms

$\mathbf{S}$hirley Murillo grew up in southern Florida, where hurricane warnings are common. In August 1992, Hurricane Andrew struck southern Florida. This storm, a Category 5 hurricane, was much stronger than most other hurricanes. It caused severe damage and hardship throughout the area. More than twenty people died. Thousands of homes were destroyed. After the storm passed, Shirley observed the destruction it had caused and realized how important it is to be able to forecast hurricanes. This experience, combined with her interest in science, motivated Shirley to want to study hurricanes and their deadly winds.

As a senior in high school, Shirley completed a year-long internship at the National Oceanic and Atmospheric Administration (NOAA). There, she worked in the Hurricane Research Division and helped scientists in their study of these monster storms. Shirley loved her job so much that she worked many more hours than she was expected to.

These days, Shirley still spends a lot of time at the Hurricane Research Division where she works as a Research Meteorologist for NOAA. In the lab, she uses computers to analyze hurricane wind data. Much of the information comes from aircraft that fly into the storms. Additional data comes from satellites, ships, and buoys. The results of Shirley's work are input into computer models that the National Hurricane Center uses to study the potential development and track of a hurricane. By studying these computerized simulations, forecasters can decide where and when to issue hurricane watches and warnings.

In this mission you will see how scientists measure the intensity of a hurricane. You will learn about the dangers that monster storms can pose. You will also learn what you can do to prepare for and survive severe weather, wherever you live.

 Mission 5 Briefing Video See how Shirley uses her knowledge of hurricane winds to help communities stay prepared and keep people safe.

NOAA-11
8/24/92
4:40 PM
EDT
Visible &
Infrared
Composite
Hurricane
Andrew

Naples

Miami

NOAA

NOAA Photo Library/Online World Collection

▲ Hurricane Andrew churns in the Gulf of Mexico on August 24, 1992, hours after ravaging the southern tip of Florida where it caused most of its $26 billion in total damage.

Mission Briefing

The Hazards of Hurricanes

Hurricanes are powerful storms that form over warm ocean water, far from human settlements. Long before a storm makes landfall, modern storm-tracking technology provides the time and tools to anticipate the hurricane's behavior and assess its potential threat to people and property. Even ships at sea are safer now than ever before. Captains make use of forecasts and satellite data to chart courses that will steer them away from the fiercest winds and high waves.

The strength of a hurricane is related to the air pressure in the eye of the storm. The strongest hurricanes generally have very low air pressure in their eye.

Hurricane Wilma, which formed in 2005, had an extremely low air pressure of 882 millibars—the lowest recorded for an Atlantic hurricane. Wind speed varies within the regions of a hurricane. The strongest winds usually occur near the eyewall, where air pressure values change rapidly. The maximum intensity of winds in

Saffir-Simpson Scale—Tropical Storm Air Pressure Measurement							
	Tropical Depression	Tropical Storm	Saffir-Simpson Hurricane Potential Damage Scale (5 categories)				
			1	2	3	4	5
Barometric Pressure (in millibars)			≥ 980 mb	979–965 mb	964–945 mb	944–920 mb	< 920 mb
Wind Speeds	< 63 km/h < 39 mph < 34 kt	63–118 km/h 39–73 mph 34–63 kt	119–153 km/h 74–95 mph 64–82 kt	154–177 km/h 96–110 mph 83–95 kt	178–209 km/h 111–130 mph 96–113 kt	210–249 km/h 131–155 mph 114–135 kt	> 249 km/h > 155 mph > 135 kt
Storm Surge			1.0–1.7 m (3–5 ft)	1.8–2.6 m (6–8 ft)	2.7–3.8 m (9–12 ft)	3.9–5.6 m (13–18 ft)	≥ 5.7 m (19 ft)

▲ The Saffir-Simpson Scale is used to estimate the potential property damage and flooding expected from a hurricane.

Wilma's eyewall exceeded 275 km/h (171 mph). Wind speed gradually decreases outward from the eyewall. In the Northern Hemisphere, winds on the right side of a hurricane (with respect to its path) are usually stronger than winds on the left side of the storm. The strongest winds occur on the right side because in this region the horizontal winds that blow the storm forward are combining with the counterclockwise whirling winds within the storm.

If you listen to NOAA Weather Radio or other weather broadcasts, you are probably aware that the **Saffir-Simpson Scale** rates a hurricane's intensity. Developed in 1969, this scale assigns a hurricane to one of five categories based on its wind speed.

Similar to the Enhanced-Fujita Scale, which rates tornadoes *after* they touch down, the Saffir-Simpson rating system began as a way to rate damage after a storm made landfall. Now, after many years of comparative storm observations, forecasters can categorize the hurricanes *before* they make landfall. In addition to wind speed, the Saffir-Simpson Scale predicts the rise in sea level caused by the arrival of the storm. But be prepared for changes! As hurricanes strengthen and weaken, their category rating is updated to reflect those changes in the storm's intensity.

Although wind causes much damage during a hurricane, water can become an even greater threat to life and property. The rush of water driven to shore by the storm's forceful winds is called a **storm surge**. As wind speeds increase, water within a surge can build to a height above the roof level of small dwellings. This wall of water, highest where the eye of the storm makes landfall, can impact 80–160 km (50–99 mi) of shoreline.

Dropsonde

A dropsonde, whose technical name is *airborne vertical atmospheric profiling system*, is a canister of weather sensors released from specially equipped aircraft. The dropsonde deploys a parachute that slows its descent through the weather system as it falls to Earth. Weather sensors contained in the dropsonde collect data to profile the atmosphere. As the probe descends, the data is transmitted to the computer system carried onboard the mission aircraft.

Diameter: 6.98 cm (2.75 in.)

Height: 40.6 cm (16 in.)

Mass (weight): 390 g (0.86 lb)

Operational ceiling: can be released from altitudes as high as 24 km (15 mi)

Electronic sensors: weather sensors that measure air pressure, temperature, and humidity. A Global Positioning System (GPS) receiver collects positional data used to determine horizontal wind speed and direction.

Transmitter: data collected by the sensors and GPS is transmitted every 0.5 seconds to the monitoring aircraft. The transmitter in the dropsonde canister has a range of 325 km (202 mi).

- The parachute that slows the dropsonde's fall to Earth is shaped like an upside-down, four-sided pyramid. The shape helps stabilize the descent, reducing the side-to-side sway of a standard parachute design.
- When released from an altitude of 12 km (7.5 mi), the dropsonde reaches the ground in about 12 minutes.
- Dropsondes were developed in the early 1970s and updated in 1987 with new, lighter electronics and digital data collection instruments.
- In addition to studying hurricanes, dropsondes are also used to profile the atmosphere of severe thunderstorms and winter storm systems.

Risk Assessment

The data that Shirley Murillo collects helps forecasters at NOAA's National Hurricane Center decide when and where a monster storm will most likely hit. But more importantly, it helps them issue more accurate warnings to affected communities about the storm's approach, track, and the potential damage it will cause. This data is also used by the Federal Emergency Management Agency (FEMA) to create risk maps that show where risks are greatest for various monster storms. These maps help the federal government decide where to put vital resources and how to help people in affected areas.

When a hurricane strikes a community, that community's emergency planners use data like the data Shirley provides to decide how best to offer help, especially to those in the most urgent need.

In this lab, you will analyze a map of recent hurricane activity along the Gulf and Atlantic coasts, and a risk assessment map. You will then be in charge of deciding how a community can best use emergency response teams, financial resources, and reserves of supplies to prepare for the impact of a monster storm.

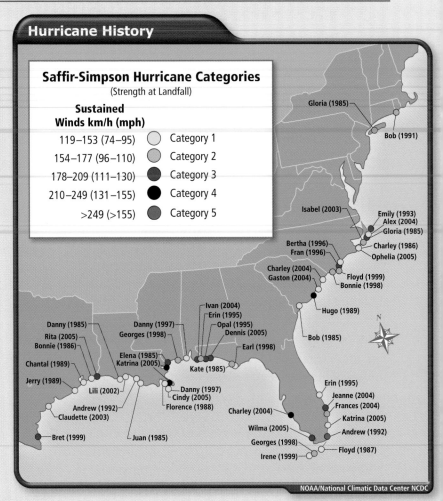

Hurricane History

Saffir-Simpson Hurricane Categories
(Strength at Landfall)

Sustained Winds km/h (mph)

119–153 (74–95)	Category 1
154–177 (96–110)	Category 2
178–209 (111–130)	Category 3
210–249 (131–155)	Category 4
>249 (>155)	Category 5

NOAA/National Climatic Data Center NCDC

Materials
- Lab 1 Data Sheet

Make Observations
Use the Hurricane History map and the Risk Assessment map to answer the following questions.

1 What category of hurricane is most common for the coastal United States?

2 Which state has experienced the most hurricanes? Why is this state so prone to hurricanes?

3 Using your knowledge of hurricane development, explain why the northeast coast of the United States experiences fewer hurricanes than other areas.

4 Based on the Risk Assessment map, if you live in the state of Texas, what is your greatest risk? Note that each risk is indicated at a statewide level. Do you expect the level of risk for hurricanes in Texas, for example, to be the same throughout the entire state? Explain.

5 Which states within the continental United States are at highest risk for both hurricanes and tornadoes?

Develop a Plan
For your city, town, or community, research a type of monster storm event that could possibly impact you. Using information from your own research, *www.fema.gov*, and *www.noaa.gov*, develop a response plan to help your local government and citizens prepare for a monster storm. Include the following information in your plan:

FEMA

- What is the population of the region included in your plan?

- What emergency response resources are available (police, fire, hospitals, etc.)?

- Does your city or region have a Red Cross center (or similar agency)? What kind of emergency preparedness information can they provide?

- If people must evacuate, how will an evacuation order and evacuation route information be communicated to them?

- What facilities can be used as shelters and where are they located?

- What should individuals do to prepare for a storm (stockpile water and emergency supplies, for example)?

- How will you rescue stranded individuals and provide critical care to sick and elderly?

- What resources and tools would be required for cleaning up and removing debris?

- How will you provide relief resources (food, water, clothing) after the storm?

States with Highest Incidence of:

	Flooding		Tornadoes
	Thunderstorms		Hurricanes

- How will you provide emergency sanitation and restore sanitary conditions?

- Are there any other important considerations for this type of emergency event in your particular community?

Extension

1 When planning urban construction or development, what consideration should city planners and engineers give to natural hazards such as monster storms?

2 How is wildlife affected by monster storms in your area?

 Journal Question How do human activities, such as land use and urban growth, factor into the damage that can result from a monster storm?

Team Highlight

The Argonauts did a lot of work that made them excited to learn more about weather and hurricanes. Their mission was to measure four parameters: ambient temperature, dew point, wind speed, and wind direction. Here the Argonauts are taking wind samples.

Storm surges are especially dangerous along the southern coast of the United States. In this area, the land rises only slightly above sea level, making the shoreline extremely vulnerable. As a result, it is possible for a moderate storm surge to spill over levees and flood-walls. With enough force, storm surges can even demolish the vertical barriers constructed to contain rising floodwaters.

Suppose that you knew a hurricane was on the way. What sort of storm surge should you expect? The approximate height of a storm surge can be inferred by the hurricane's assigned category on the Saffir-Simpson Hurricane Scale. In general, a Category 1 storm will have a storm surge that is from 1.0–1.7 m (3–5 ft) above the normal level of the tide. A Category 2 storm will have a surge that can rise 1.8–2.6 m (6–8 ft) above normal. Category 5 hurricanes can produce storm surges of over 5.7 m (19 ft).

The final height to which the storm surge will rise is greatly influenced by the shape of the coastline. For example, if the rising water is funneled into a narrow passageway, it piles up, creating an even higher surge. This is often observed in narrow inlets or bays. Another factor is the time of tide when the storm surge arrives. A surge will have less impact if it arrives at low tide than at high tide. The most destructive surges arrive during spring high tides, when the water is already well above the average tide level.

The high water, waves, and swift currents associated with a storm surge can erode barriers and rip structures apart. Buildings that remain standing sustain heavy water damage. A storm surge may also take many lives, because escaping from one can be quite difficult. Sometimes people take refuge in their homes. As the water level rises, they may eventually

Storm Surge

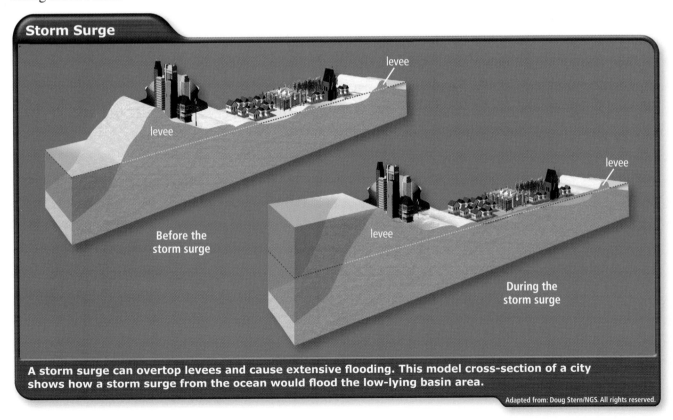

levee

levee

levee

levee

Before the storm surge

During the storm surge

A storm surge can overtop levees and cause extensive flooding. This model cross-section of a city shows how a storm surge from the ocean would flood the low-lying basin area.

▲ This house is being raised 3.4 m (11 ft) to minimize further flood damage from hurricanes.

become trapped in the attic with no means of escape. Often, rescuers must cut through the roof to reach the trapped victims.

Most people do not realize that just a few centimeters of swiftly moving water can knock them off their feet. A mere 15 cm (6 in.) of moving water can sweep a car off the road. Many drownings occur when people are trapped in cars caught in floodwaters. In fact, since 1970, more than half of all hurricane-related deaths have resulted from flooding.

A surge blown ashore by the high winds is not the only type of flooding that can occur during a hurricane. Heavy rain may cause rivers to overflow their banks, producing flood conditions many hundreds of miles inland. Like their coastal counterparts, these inland floods are destructive and dangerous.

Some hurricanes produce other violent storms—tornadoes. Tornadoes sometimes form in the outer edge of a hurricane as it makes landfall. Tornadoes can continue to develop for days after landfall and for long distances inland. Hurricane Beulah, which made landfall along the Texas coast in 1967, spawned an amazing 115 tornadoes!

Preparing for a Monster Storm

Suppose you were told that your home could lose electricity for a day. What would you do? You might make a list of your home's electrical appliances and devices and consider the consequences of these items being without power for 24 hours. Is the operation of any particular item essential to maintaining your home or your ability to remain in that space? If so, does it have a battery or generator backup? Would a temporary shutdown create any hazardous situation? After considering questions like these, you would need to decide on a plan of action. Doing so would prepare you to deal with the situation as best you could. That is what being prepared is all about.

Preparedness is also essential in the effort to protect lives and property from the rage of a monster storm and its aftermath. Before the storm strikes, you need to consider seriously the impact of its arrival. How should you deal with the danger that it poses?

Although each storm is different, certain strategies apply to almost every situation. These preparedness strategies are presented in the pages that follow.

Storm Surge!

As a student, Shirley Murillo was inspired to learn about hurricanes when she witnessed the damage produced by these monster storms. Now, she and other scientists at NOAA's Hurricane Research Division use computer models, satellite data, and information collected from a variety of other sources to help people on land prepare for approaching storms.

During a hurricane, one of the greatest threats to life and property is a storm surge. As hurricanes move toward land, they push a mass of water in front of them. When this wall of water reaches land, it can have very destructive and often deadly consequences.

To contain storm surges, embankments called *levees* are built along shorelines. Most levees are made from earthen materials that are piled high along the water's edge. Sometimes a concrete or metal barrier called a floodwall offers added protection. As long as these upright structures remain intact, they can contain rising water levels. However, if they are breached or destroyed, there is nothing left to hold back a major flood!

In addition to engineered walls and levees, there are natural systems in place that help reduce storm damage. Along a coastline, for example, healthy ecosystems help stabilize the land. Coastal wetlands can help absorb water from storm surges and flooding. Healthy vegetation retains the soil, reducing weathering and erosion. Natural barriers can absorb the initial brunt of the storm, lessening the force that reaches populated areas.

Builders can construct houses to resist hurricane winds and storm surges. Raising a dwelling or placing it on stilts reduces the possibility of damage caused by rising waters. In this lab, you will build a model of a city and try to protect it from any incoming storm surge. Can you minimize the loss of life and property resulting from a monster storm?

Materials
- **Lab 2 Data Sheet**
- **baking dish, 9 × 13 × 2 or larger**
- **waterproof clay**
- **small gravel (up to 3-cm-dia.)**
- **sand**
- **water**
- **toothpicks**

Lab Prep

1. When planning for storm surge, why is it important to know the topography of the area?

2. If a storm approaches an area having a narrow inlet or bay, why will the storm surge be higher than it would be if the inlet or bay were a wide one?

3. Why would a Category 4 storm cause more storm surge than a Category 2 storm in the same area?

4. Explain why flooding from rainfall can be just as damaging as a storm surge.

5. How does wind contribute to both storm surge and rain damage?

Make Observations

You are going to construct a model coastal area that will be susceptible to a storm surge. Discuss with your teacher and your classmates the characteristics of the topography, buildings, and infrastructure that one might find in a coastal region. These could include low-sloped shorelines, unprotected harbors, and waterfront structures.

1. Using your clay and small gravel, construct a model shoreline in the baking dish. Your model will have a vertical scale of 1 cm = 2 m, and a horizontal scale of 1 cm = 100 m. Explain why you think these scales are different.

2. Add a small amount of water to the dish so that it begins to overlap the shoreline. Use a toothpick to etch this waterline into the clay. What does this line represent? Draw a topographic map of your model coastline that shows the contour of the water's edge. Be sure to indicate the scale of your map.

3. Use a pen to mark 1/2-cm increments on the length of another toothpick, and stick it into the clay at the edge of the water. You will use this to measure storm surge levels. What is this height in meters of a Category 1 storm surge? Use the Saffir-Simpson Scale on page 89 as a guide. Now add water to your model until the sea level reaches the height of a Category 1 surge. Etch the new waterline in the clay. Then, draw a new contour line on your map that shows the water level for a Category 1 storm surge.

④ Repeat step 3 for Category 2 through Category 5 storm surges. Be sure to etch each new water level in the model, and draw and label each one on your map.

⑤ Now empty all the water from the baking dish and build a levee that will protect your coastal region. Explain your decision about where you choose to build the barrier and why. Make a prediction about the severity of storm that it will protect against. Now test your model. Does your levee function the way you expected? Why or why not?

Interpret Data

① The primary use of your coastal region could be any of several things. Suppose that it is used for either beach recreation and tourism, commercial fishing and shipping, or luxury residential living. How would each of these different uses affect your decision about where to build a barrier or levee system? Explain each case.

② The levee system for the City of New Orleans was built to withstand a Category 3 storm. What factors do you think were considered in making this choice, rather than building a levee that could withstand a Category 4 or 5 storm?

Extension

The City of New Orleans is constructed in a bowl-like depression between the Mississippi River and Lake Pontchartrain. Research the layout of the city and make a model of it. Be sure to include levees and floodwalls that hold back the waters of the lake and river. Also indicate spillways that connect them. The Army Corps of Engineers designed the spillways to carry water from the river to the lake. Add water to test your model. Use your observations to propose a long-term reconstruction plan for the city.

 Journal Question Describe some of the conditions that limit a city's ability to prepare for storm surge. Why are these conditions limiting?

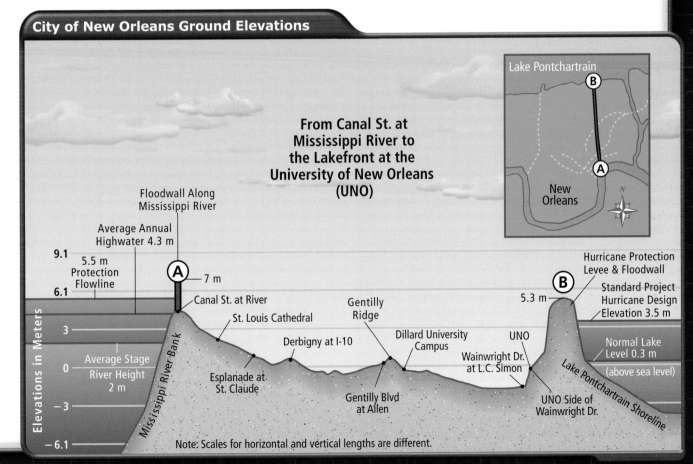

City of New Orleans Ground Elevations

From Canal St. at Mississippi River to the Lakefront at the University of New Orleans (UNO)

Note: Scales for horizontal and vertical lengths are different.

CASSANDRA SANTAMARIA
Student Argonaut, California

Student Argonaut Cassandra Santamaria and Host Researcher Shirley Murillo take wind speed measurements in Miami to identify weather patterns and forecast potentially severe weather.

The Argonauts debriefed with Shirley on their data collection from their field work. They discovered that their collection of data was a very important part of understanding monster storms. Shirley explained that this information enables meteorologists to issue earlier warnings and towns to begin more timely emergency response.

Fast Fact

Naming tropical storms and hurricanes has changed many times over the years. From 1941 until 1951 and resuming in 1953 until 1978, Atlantic tropical storms and hurricanes were identified using women's names. In 1979 men's and women's names were alternated in distinguishing Atlantic and eastern Pacific tropical storms and hurricanes. Today, name lists include French, Spanish, Dutch, and English names. Also the letters Q, X , Y, and Z are not included because of the scarcity of names starting with these letters.

In 2005, so many storms occurred in the Atlantic that the last storms of the season had to be named according to the Greek alphabet. These storms were called Alpha, Beta, Gamma, Delta, Epsilon, and lastly Zeta, which formed on December 30, 2005.

Notable hurricanes before 1941 were sometimes named for the date and point of landfall. Two great hurricanes to impact the United States were the Galveston Hurricane of 1900, and the Hurricane of 1938, also called the *Long Island Express*. Scientists use a variety of sources to research the history of hurricanes including historical records, diaries, local oral history, and ships' logs.

Hurricane Preparedness

What are hurricane watches and warnings?

Hurricane watches and warnings are advisories issued by the National Weather Service. Most often, they are communicated to the general public through television and radio broadcasts. As a hurricane is approaching landfall, more data is available to forecasters to predict its track and intensity. If you live in a region that could be affected by the storm, be sure to keep a radio or television tuned to local weather announcements for the most current information.

A **watch** is issued when hurricane conditions are possible within the next 36 hours. During a hurricane watch, people should prepare their homes against possible damage. They should also review their evacuation plan. A **warning** is issued when hurricane conditions are expected within 24 hours. If a warning is given, people should complete their storm preparations. They should evacuate the area if told to do so.

What should I do before and during a hurricane?

If you live in an area affected by hurricanes, there are many things you can do to prepare before hurricane season begins. Remember that when a monster storm arrives, there is a good chance that you will lose electrical power, as well as telephone and Internet service. You may even have to leave your home for a time. That is why you need to pack items that will help you survive both the immediate storm and its possible after effects.

Hurricane Preparedness Kit

- ☐ Bottled water (3 gallons, about 12 liters, per person minimum)
- ☐ First-aid kit
- ☐ Medicine
- ☐ Extra clothing and bedding
- ☐ Food that does not need refrigeration or cooking
- ☐ Can opener for cans
- ☐ Cash
- ☐ Flashlight
- ☐ Battery-powered NOAA Weather Radio or portable radio
- ☐ Extra batteries for flashlight and radio
- ☐ Important papers (identification and emergency contacts)
- ☐ Transportation plans in case of evacuation

Put together a hurricane preparedness kit and make sure that everyone in your household knows where the kit is kept. If a hurricane watch is issued, listen to broadcasts on NOAA Weather Radio or on commercial radio or television for weather updates. Cover windows and doors with sheets of plywood. Tie down or store trash cans and other items that could blow away during the storm. Learn evacuation routes and find out where emergency shelters are located.

Review your emergency plan with others in the family, and have your hurricane kit ready. If a warning is issued, stay calm. Listen to the radio or watch television for information about the storm's behavior and expected arrival. Follow the instructions given by officials. If you are asked to evacuate the area, do so immediately. Your family should move a safe distance inland and find a place to stay. If you are not all traveling together, agree on a place where you will meet. Tell someone who is not in the hurricane warning area where you will be staying and how they can contact you.

If you are not told to leave or if you are unable to leave and your house is well constructed, stay inside. For a supply of fresh drinking water, fill the bathtub with water. Unplug small appliances. Stay in a room

▼ Hurricane evacuees waiting to leave New Orleans

Marty Bahamonde/FEMA Photo Library

▼ A hurricane's devastating aftermath

Mark Wolfe/FEMA Photo Library

near the center of the building away from doors and windows. If you must leave your house, find the nearest emergency shelter. Remember to take your hurricane kit with you.

What should I do after the hurricane has passed?

After the hurricane has passed, stay informed about the weather. Large volumes of rain have probably caused flooding. Stay away from floodwaters. Do not attempt to walk or drive through flowing water. When the area is declared safe, survey any damage. Stay away from downed power lines, and use water from your tap only after you are told that it is safe to do so.

Tornado Preparedness

Although tornadoes can form throughout the year and have been recorded in every state, there are patterns to their formation. In the United States, most tornadoes form east of the Rocky Mountains in a region rightly named Tornado Alley. In southern states, tornadoes are more likely to appear from the end of winter through late spring. In northern states, they tend to appear in late spring through early summer.

▼ Tornado funnel cloud in the early stages of formation

NOAA Photo Library/NSSL

While weather and news broadcasts will warn of conditions in which a tornado may form, these monster storms sometimes appear suddenly with little or no warning. Forecasters are generally good at identifying the weather conditions that might produce a tornado. The National Weather Service, a division of NOAA, will issue a tornado watch when the data they are observing indicates these atmospheric conditions exist. When a watch is issued, you need to be ready to take shelter if the storm moves into your area.

If the storm conditions grow worse, a tornado warning will be issued. This means a tornado or funnel cloud has been spotted. Listen to the weather warnings and follow emergency broadcast instructions. Quickly find a safe place that is indoors and away from glass windows and doors. Plan ahead and identify a tornado shelter such as a basement or nearby sturdy building that can offer protection from the violent winds.

Many years ago people believed they should open a window in their home if a tornado was approaching, thinking that a house could otherwise explode due to pressure differences caused by the tornado winds. Science has shown that this belief is not true. Keep your windows closed to minimize damage to the interior of the house. Most damage to homes, both inside and out, is the result of flying debris. In addition, it is best to be dressed in sturdy shoes and outdoor clothing. If a tornado strikes your area, rugged clothes will protect you more during and after the storm.

If you are in a car when a tornado approaches, get out and find other safe cover. Tornadoes can toss cars, so they are not a safe place to stay. Find shelter in a sturdy building. Do not try to outrun a nearby tornado. Its direction and speed can change in an instant. It is also unsafe to remain in a mobile home or trailer. Unlike more massive and sturdier buildings, mobile homes and trailers are more apt to be tossed or torn apart by the tornado's high winds. Seek shelter elsewhere.

Even very large buildings, such as shopping malls, auditoriums, and cafeterias, do not make good shelters. Their wide-span roofs are more likely to sustain damage from high winds than the roofs of smaller buildings.

After the tornado, beware of hazards such as downed electrical lines or ruptured gas lines. If you spot a problem, stay away, and report the damage to the authorities. Wear sturdy shoes and clothing to protect yourself from scratches and cuts from debris. Watch out for shattered glass that might litter the

▲ Dramatic cloud-to-ground lightning illuminates the night sky. Thunderstorms can present many hazards including lightning strikes, floods, and damaging winds.

landscape. Do not enter structurally damaged buildings until they are inspected and declared safe.

Once the storm passes, be prepared to help with cleanup, but stay out of the way of emergency responders. They will need to coordinate help for many affected people and make decisions about how to best deal with the many tasks of recovery and aid to victims. Recovery from a storm may involve many personnel and volunteers from local, state, and federal organizations and agencies. Staying informed of the assistance available through these organizations and offices can help speed the recovery of a community.

Tornado Preparedness Kit

To be ready for a tornado event, you can assemble a tornado safety kit that includes these essential items:

- Flashlight
- Battery-powered NOAA Weather Radio
- Extra batteries for flashlight and radio
- Cell phone
- First-aid kit and prescription drugs
- Bottled water, canned food, high-energy snacks
- Manual can opener
- Sturdy shoes
- Outdoor clothing
- Blankets

Thunderstorm Preparedness

Thunderstorms comprise many dangerous and potentially lethal weather elements. These storms are relatively common; and, while they are not as strong as hurricanes or tornadoes, thunderstorms can still be life-threatening or cause serious injury.

Lightning is probably the best known hazard of thunderstorms. However, thunderstorms can produce other dangerous conditions such as flash flooding, hail, and tornadoes. In fact, most deaths associated with thunderstorms are not the result of lightning strikes. They are caused by the rapidly rising water of flash floods.

Although the rainfall can be extreme, precipitation often occurs in intense bursts of downpours, each lasting several minutes. Precipitation from a thunderstorm rarely lasts more than an hour. However, in this short time, flash floods can occur if heavy rain falls so rapidly that it cannot be absorbed by the ground. The runoff flows downhill and collects quickly in low-lying areas. During a flash flood, a river of water can appear to come from out of nowhere in a matter of seconds.

Severe thunderstorms are monster weather systems having one or more of the following characteristics: hail at least 2 cm (4/5 in.) in diameter; winds in excess of 93.3 km/h (58 mph); or funnel clouds or tornadoes.

To make your property safer in the event of severe thunderstorms, make sure that dead trees or rotting branches don't pose a threat to the house, cars, or other structures like sheds, garages, patios, and decks. In the wild winds of a storm, falling branches and toppling trees can crash through houses or crush cars.

If severe thunderstorms are forecast for your area, listen to broadcasts on NOAA Weather Radio or on commercial radio or television stations. Be sure that your radio is battery-powered and that you have an extra supply of batteries, just in case there is a power outage.

Seek shelter inside a building or some other sturdy structure. Make sure that outdoor objects are secured and will not be tossed by the storm's violent winds. Unplug electrical and electronic devices. They can be damaged by the power surges caused by lightning strikes.

If you are in a vehicle when a severe storm strikes, remain inside the vehicle unless it is a convertible. The metal roof of a hard-top vehicle completes an "electrical cage" that helps protect those inside from electrocution caused by lightning strikes. Because a convertible lacks a metal roof, it does not offer the same protective space.

Lightning can strike over 16 km (10 mi) from the downpours of a thunderstorm. If you hear thunder, it is best to seek the safety of a car or a building immediately. Avoid high ground because lighting usually strikes the highest objects in the vicinity of the storm. Therefore, do not take cover under a tree; get inside a house or other building for shelter. Avoid open fields, golf courses, and beaches. If you're in a boat, head for safety in the nearest harbor. If lightning strikes are nearby and it is impossible to find good cover, you can crouch or lay down on the ground to reduce your chances of being struck.

Do not expect rubber-soled shoes to protect you. The relatively thin layer of rubber on the bottom of a shoe is not enough insulating material to protect you from the awesome electrical current of a lightning strike. If someone is struck by lightning and you are available to assist them, it is safe to touch the injured person. There is no danger of "residual" electricity in their body. As lightning strikes an object or the ground, the electrical charge continues to flow into the ground. The electricity does not remain in the object it hits. Therefore, it is entirely safe to touch or to offer CPR or other types of medical attention to someone who has been struck by lightning.

Winter Storm Preparedness

A winter storm warning alerts you that heavy snowfall or extreme cold is headed your way. Unlike a storm watch, which identifies the possibility of a winter storm, a warning informs you that the storm will arrive shortly. You can find out more about the approaching weather by listening to NOAA Weather Radio or to local radio or television broadcasts.

The National Weather Service will issue a blizzard warning for a severe winter storm if it meets several criteria. A winter storm is categorized as a **blizzard** if it comes with high winds in excess of 56 km/h (35 mph), dangerous wind chill, and heavy falling and/or blowing snow that will last for at least three hours.

During a severe winter storm it is best to remain inside and keep from doing any unnecessary traveling. Keep warm and prepare for the loss of electrical power, telephone service, and heat. To conserve heat, close off unneeded rooms. If you have a cell phone,

Fast Fact

Snow events known as "lake-effect snow" have a very intense and localized impact on many areas around the Great Lakes in the winter. These storms can last for days and deliver several feet of snow in sharply defined regions, called snowbelts, just inland from the shore. Lake-effect snow, falling at rates as much as 15 cm (6 in.) per hour, is created when cold arctic air sweeps down from Canada over the relatively warm waters of the Great Lakes. It picks up moisture and almost immediately deposits it as snow. When there is a very sharp contrast in temperature between the air in upper elevations and the surface air near the lakes, this added instability can cause a rare event called thundersnow, which is snow accompanied by thunder and lightning.

▲ Strong winds and heavy snowfall can produce blinding conditions in a blizzard.

use it only when essential in order to conserve its battery. Make sure you have access to shovels to begin digging out when the storm is over.

After the storm, continue to listen to radio or television reports for information updates, road conditions, school and office closings, and other affected services. Look around your property for damage that may have occurred. Remove snow from walkways and from around furnace vents and laundry vents so that these vents can operate freely. If you see downed electrical lines, stay away and contact authorities immediately. Make sure water pipes are not frozen. You can use a hair dryer to thaw pipes if they do freeze.

Contact neighbors to make sure that they are all right, particularly if there are infants, elderly people, or people with disabilities who live near you. They may require additional help in dealing with conditions brought on by a winter storm.

When shoveling snow, do not overdo it. In some individuals, the physical exertion can lead to serious injuries, including cardiac arrest. You may want to have a supply of sand to spread on walkways and driveways for better traction. A supply of road salt can also come in handy to accelerate melting or prevent the formation of ice.

Avoid traveling during and after a winter storm until you know that conditions have improved and roads are passable. If you must travel by car, let someone know where you are headed, what route you plan to take, and when you expect to arrive. Keep a storm supply kit in the trunk, and keep the car's gas tank full. If you get stranded during a storm, stay with the car; do not try to walk to safety. Tie a brightly colored cloth to the antenna for rescuers to see. Start the car and use the heater for about ten minutes every hour, and keep your arms and legs moving to stay warm. Be sure that the exhaust pipe outside the car stays clear so that deadly carbon monoxide does not back up into the car. Wait for emergency assistance to arrive.

Winter Storm Preparedness Kit

To be ready for the winter storm season, you can assemble a storm safety kit that includes these items:

- ☐ Flashlight
- ☐ Battery-powered NOAA Weather Radio
- ☐ Extra batteries for flashlight and radio
- ☐ Cell phone
- ☐ First-aid kit and prescription drugs
- ☐ Bottled water, canned food, high-energy snacks
- ☐ Manual can opener
- ☐ Layers of warm clothing
- ☐ Hats, mittens, and boots
- ☐ Extra blankets

▲ In 1988 widespread drought in the United States resulted in economic losses of over $60 billion.

Drought Preparedness

Unlike the sudden and powerful arrival of most monster storms, a **drought** results from a prolonged period of below-normal rainfall. To prepare for a drought, it is critically important to conserve water resources. Doing so will minimize the effects of drought on your community.

Because water is such a precious resource, drought conditions require that we pay real attention to conserving water. Conservation involves using fresh water as efficiently as possible and reusing it when practical. This may mean not watering your grass as long or as often, or not washing the car. It means saving water for drinking, cleaning, and cooking. Opportunities to reduce the use of water and to recycle it are key components in water conservation.

Beyond reducing the available water supply for human consumption, there can be other serious effects of drought. Over a long period, below-normal rainfall can adversely affect plants and livestock. Crops can be damaged or lost. Without sufficient rainfall, the threat of forest fire or wildfire increases. Livestock can suffer from dehydration, with deadly consequences.

Water Conservation Activities and Practices

Indoor
- Fix all leaky and dripping faucets.
- Make sure that your toilet does not leak or that its handle does not get stuck.
- Reuse water when practical. For example, water to be discarded could be used to water plants.
- Use a low-volume shower head. Take shorter showers.
- Do not let the water run while brushing your teeth or washing your face.
- Use kitchen dishwashers and laundry washers only when you have full loads.

Outdoor
- Plant drought resistant native plants.
- Water the grass only when absolutely necessary. Avoid overwatering.
- Pay attention to local restrictions on times when lawns can be watered.
- Make sure that hose connections are tight and do not leak.
- Turn off hoses and spigots when not in use.
- Avoid sprinklers that create a fine mist that evaporates before reaching the grass.
- Make sure that the water you spray on the lawn wets only the lawn.
- Wash your car on the lawn.

Flood Preparedness

A **flood** is an unusually high flow, overflow, or inundation of water. A flood can take several hours or days to develop near or downstream from a precipitation event. A flash flood, however, can occur within minutes! When a flash flood watch is issued, be prepared to evacuate the area immediately. The best way to be ready for a flood or a flash flood is to plan ahead. Know the flood risks in the area where you live, and assemble a disaster supply kit.

If a flood watch is issued, move valuable items in your home to higher floors. Bring loose outdoor items like lawn furniture, grills, and trash cans inside. When a flood warning is issued, listen to NOAA Weather Radio or other radio and television broadcasts to keep informed on what to do and when to evacuate. Be prepared to turn off electrical power, gas, and water supplies before evacuating. Sanitize sinks and bathtubs with bleach, then fill them with clean water in case your water supply becomes contaminated by the flood. Also fill plastic bottles and jugs with clean water. You should try to have a three- to five-day supply for your household.

If ordered, evacuate to higher ground, following official instructions, observing barricades, and following posted evacuation routes. Never ignore an evacuation order, and only take essential supplies with you. If your car stalls in rapidly rising floodwater, abandon it if you can do so safely. Rushing water as little as 10 cm (4 in.) deep can knock a person down and sweep them away.

After the flood, do not return to the evacuated area until authorities give the okay to return. Do not drink tap water until you know it is safe. Floods can cause sewer systems to overflow, contaminating both the floodwaters and possibly freshwater sources. Throw away all food that may have come in contact with flood or storm water. Use caution while assessing damage and cleaning up in areas like basements that may still have standing water. Stay away from downed power lines, electrical wires in water, unsafe structures and stagnant water.

If you have to clean up after a flood, be prepared to disinfect the materials you work with and wash yourself thoroughly. Bacteria, mold, viruses, and agricultural and industrial waste in unsanitary flood water can make you sick if you do not take proper precautions.

Also, protect yourself from animal-related hazards after a flood disaster. Wild animals will have been displaced from their homes in a flood. Be prepared to encounter animals that live in your area but might, under normal circumstances, not be a problem for you. Avoid wild and stray animals, and call local animal control authorities to handle them. Remove any dead animals from your property according to guidelines supplied by animal control. Dispose of garbage and debris as soon as possible to avoid attracting wild animals looking for food and new shelter.

Flood Preparedness Kit

To be ready for a flood, you can assemble a flood safety kit that includes these items:

- ☐ Flashlight
- ☐ Battery-powered radio, ideally a NOAA Weather Radio
- ☐ Extra batteries for flashlight and radio
- ☐ Cell phone
- ☐ Bottled water, canned food, and high-energy snacks
- ☐ Manual can opener
- ☐ Water-purifying supplies (chlorine or iodine tablets)
- ☐ First-aid supplies and prescription medicines
- ☐ Written instructions for the correct way to turn off gas and electricity if authorities advise you to do so
- ☐ Evacuation plan that includes where to go and how you can be contacted
- ☐ Clothing, including rain gear and boots
- ☐ Rubber gloves
- ☐ Personal hygiene supplies

▼ Flooding caused by the heavy rains of a hurricane can wash cars off the road.

Marvin Nauman/FEMA Photo Library

Build a Better Building

Now that you have been fully briefed on monster storms, it is time to complete your assignment. Recall that your mission is to *protect life and minimize the loss of vital assets before, during, and after a storm*.

When Shirley Murillo is analyzing her data, she creates a wind field map. This map displays characteristics of winds within the hurricane. By analyzing this pattern of winds, Shirley can help storm planners make better decisions about how to minimize the damage and injuries caused by monster storms.

In this field assignment, you will learn how Shirley creates a wind field map from data. As you will discover, the task requires knowledge of weather symbols, maps, the Saffir-Simpson Scale, and hurricane behavior. You will follow Shirley's procedure to produce your own wind field map. You will then assume the role of architect and city planner and apply what you have learned to design and construct a hurricane-proof building.

Objectives: To complete your mission, accomplish the following objectives:

- Create a wind field map, using Shirley Murillo's data.
- Construct a building that will withstand hurricane force conditions.

Mission 5 Argonaut Field Assignment Video Join the National Argonauts as they study wind fields with Shirley Murillo.

Caution! Exercise caution around the leaf blower in the Mission Challenge. Your instructor should operate the blower. Do not stand forward of the blower when it is in use.

Materials

- **Mission 5 Field Assignment Data Sheet**
- **Building materials such as these:**
  - tissue paper
  - plain white paper
  - construction paper
  - plastic wrap
  - tape
  - toothpicks
  - craft sticks
  - paper clips
  - modeling clay
- **wind data**
- **blank map**
- **12 in. × 12 in. poster board square**
- **duct tape**
- **colored pencils or crayons**

Optional:
- **leaf blower**
- **small children's pool or other basin**
- **sand and bricks**

Field Preparation

 Download the wind data from Shirley's research from the JASON Mission Center. Choose one of the two storms and plot a map of its wind field. You will use latitude and longitude to plot your data points. On page 90, the Saffir-Simpson color code is indicated in the map legend. Use these colors in your map for the different plotted values of wind speed and direction.

② What is the range of high and low wind speeds in your map? Where within the storm do these speeds exist? Describe their position in relation to the eye of the hurricane and compass direction.

③ Did one side of the hurricane have higher wind speeds than the other? If so, what is the reason for the difference?

④ Identify the Saffir-Simpson category for your hurricane, describe its areas of most intense precipitation, and the direction of its track.

Mission Challenge

You will design a house that you think will withstand hurricane force winds, rain, and flooding. Your teacher will assign you a "budget" of a limited amount of materials that you can use to design your house.

① Considering the budget and materials you can use, think about a design for your model house. Use the following questions to help you make decisions:

a. How can the structure be both strong and practical for its occupants?

b. What is more important: protection from rain or protection from wind?

c. Is there a balance between being waterproof and being wind resistant?

d. Where should windows be placed? How many?

2 Use the 12-in. square of poster board as the foundation for your house. Using other building materials as appropriate, assemble your house on this foundation, leaving the edges of the poster board exposed. The house must measure at least 15 cm (6 in.) on each side, and have at least two paper sides.

3 After your house is built, you will test your design. Bring your house outdoors. For a more realistic model, your teacher might set up a children's swimming pool with sand, bricks, and water. You could also simply place your house on a paved surface. Tape down the edges of the poster board to firmly anchor your foundation, either on bricks in the sand or on the pavement.

4 Your teacher will use the leaf blower or another wind-making device to simulate hurricane force winds. How can you simulate a Category 1 storm? How can you simulate a Category 5 storm?

5 What effect does (or would) the water have?

6 Which do you think is more destructive, the water or the wind? Why?

7 If your building has been destroyed, how could you rebuild it to enhance its safety in the event of another hurricane?

Mission Debrief

1 No design is indestructible. What were some of the trade-offs for your building design (such as safety, cost, efficiency, or appearance)?

2 If you had to do it again, would you make the same trade-offs? Why or why not?

3 Knowing what you know now about hurricanes, if you were building a home on a coastline, what guidelines would you give to the builders? Why?

4 What impact does removing trees, shrubbery, and other vegetation from coastal areas have on the extent of damage that buildings sustain in a storm?

5 What building regulations (considering cost, time, and materials needed) should cities impose to protect their citizens? Why are such regulations appropriate?

Extension

What type(s) of monster storm(s) is your area most vulnerable to experiencing? Research the building regulations for your city. Are they adequate protection against monster storms? If they are not, what would you change? Explain your answer.

 Journal Question Although they live in areas prone to storms such as hurricanes and tornadoes, many people continue to live in homes that are not built to withstand high winds and water. What can be done to protect these people and minimize the damage before, during, and after a storm?

Mark Wolfe/FEMA Photo Library

Lightning: A Monster Transfer of Energy

Kaboom! You are jolted awake by the crash of nearby thunder. As your eyes open wide, you witness a mind-boggling sight. A fireball enters through a window. About the size and shape of a basketball, it bounces off the walls of your bedroom. Then as suddenly as it appeared, it seems to leap into an electrical wall outlet and disappear. This was just *too bizarre*. It *had* to be a dream. Nothing as strange as this could ever really happen. Right? Wrong.

Not all lightning appears as bolts. One of its strangest forms is something called *ball lightning*. This electrical discharge resembles a ball of fire. Unlike an abrupt flash, ball lightning can last several seconds. In different instances, it has been observed to stand nearly still, roll along the ground, or zip though space. As you might imagine, little is known about this very rare and extraordinary type of lightning.

What Is Lightning?

Lightning is an awesome discharge of electric energy. But for most of us, that is not what our senses detect. Instead, we see the flash of light produced during this energy transformation. We also detect thunder—shock waves produced by the explosive expansion of heated air.

The discharge of lightning is a way of returning electrical stability to the air. Before the lightning bolt strikes, there is a build-up of separated negative and positive charges. When this unstable build-up grows too large, the charges will equalize through the air and we observe lightning.

Cloud-to-ground lightning begins as a small downward discharge that zigzags through the air. When it nears the ground, small positive discharges rise up to meet it. When these bolts meet, the circuit is closed. A huge flow of electricity rushes down through the electrically unstable air. The bolt is quickly followed by additional strokes, producing a strobe-like effect.

Mystery of Formation

Believe it or not, no one knows for certain how lightning begins. Some scientists think that the sun's solar wind is responsible for lightning. Bathing our planet in a stream of charged particles, the solar wind may disrupt the air's electrical balance. Other scientists think that ice crystals can cause an unstable condition in the air. Their theory is that colliding crystals within clouds separate electrical charges. Either way, it is the buildup of separated charges that leads to the formation of lightning.

Did you know?

When we think of lightning, we typically imagine those giant, crackling bolts shooting down from the sky. But most lightning bolts do not ever come near the ground! They travel between parts of the same cloud. This intra-cloud lightning looks like bright flashes that seem to light up a cloud from within.

A Tall Tale of Lightning

Benjamin Franklin studied lightning and electricity. This notion rings true. However, there is a story in which the kite he flew was struck by lightning. Well, probably not. Although this would have been an awesome sight, it would have been deadly for Mr. Franklin. Most likely, his observations on a "spark-producing" key were generated by strong electrical fields of the passing storm.

St. Elmo's Fire

Like ball lightning, St. Elmo's Fire seems like another too-strange-to-be-real phenomenon. But, it does exist! St. Elmo's Fire is a glow that appears on tall and protruding structures such as ship masts and chimneys. Scientists believe that this eerie blue light results from the electrical activity in the surrounding air.

Your Turn

You will need some gelatin powder and a balloon for this experiment. Spread a half teaspoon of gelatin powder on your desktop. Inflate a balloon and give it an electrostatic charge by rubbing it on your hair or against a wool garment. Hold the balloon just above the gelatin powder. Describe what you observe.

Join the Argonaut Adventure!

Work with and learn from the greatest explorers, scientists and researchers in the world as they engage in today's most exciting scientific explorations. JASON is always looking for Argonauts to join our science adventure. Find out here how you can be part of the team!

Local Argonauts

Local Argonauts work with other students in their classrooms and communities to explore and discover the wonders of science.

▲ Students will find complete directions and numerous helpful resources for performing the Argonaut Challenge on the **JASON Mission Center.**

Take the Argonaut Challenge

The Argonaut Challenge is an interactive science activity that gives you the opportunity to produce a multimedia project and share it with the entire JASON community. In "Create Your Local Weather Broadcast," you will collect weather data, come up with a local weather forecast, and produce a video broadcast based on your results. Your video will be displayed on the JASON Web site where the entire community of JASON Local Argonauts can watch! Are you up for the Challenge? Go to the JASON Mission Center and find out!

Start a Local Argonaut Club

Ask your teacher about starting a Local Argonaut Club in your area. Local Argonaut Clubs extend the JASON learning experience beyond the bounds of a single classroom, using local resources and information to bring JASON into your community and your own backyard. In your Local Argonaut Club, you can talk to local weather experts and storm chasers . . . or better yet, you can become a weather expert yourself!

▶ Students try their hand at building models of "hurricane-proof" houses, an activity from *Operation: Monster Storms* Mission 5. Later, they tested their designs to see how well they stood up against a leaf blower!

Begin your Argonaut Adventure at *www.jason.org*

National Argonauts

Each year, an elite group of National Argonauts ventures into the field to work with JASON Host Researchers on timely and exciting science exploration. Go online and check out their profiles, journals, photo essays, and videos from the field. See what it is like to be a National JASON Argonaut!

Interested in becoming a National Argonaut yourself, and working with the next group of JASON Host Researchers? Check online often to learn about the next opportunity and how to apply!

▲ Student Argonaut Neil Muir learning to snorkel in anticipation of his field work with JASON Host Researchers.

▲ Student Argonaut Cameron King helps mount Aerosonde on top of a truck prior to its mission launch.

▲ Host Researcher Jason Dunion and Student Argonaut Cassandra Santamaria team up on this JASON Webcast about hurricanes.

National Argonaut Alumni

Many JASON participants embody the idea of life-long learning through a journey of exploration and discovery. These Argonaut Alumni profiles show how JASON has enriched and influenced the lives of students who have gone on to be scientists, explorers, and researchers in their own right. The JASON Project helped them excel not only academically, but also in their lives at home and in their communities. Maybe JASON will make a difference in your life, too.

Read the alumni profiles by clicking **Argonaut Alumni** in the JASON Mission Center.

▲ (Left) Kristin Ludwig as a Student Argonaut in 1993 with Dr. Robert Ballard, studying deep-sea hydrothermal vents. Today, (right) Kristin is getting her Ph.D. in Oceanography from the University of Washington.

Each year JASON recruits a team of expert scientists, students, and teachers to serve on our Missions. The team includes a Host Researcher, Teacher Argonauts, and Student Argonauts like you. We also feature Argonaut Alumni—individuals who were Student Argos on previous JASON Projects and who have rejoined us for a new Mission. To learn more about the Host Researchers, login to the JASON Mission Center to read their bios and view the Meet the Researchers videos. You can also follow the Argonauts' adventures through their captivating bios, journals, and photographic galleries.

Student Argonauts

MATHEUS DENARDO
Ohio
Student Argonaut, Mission 3

Matheus was born in Campinas, San Paulo, Brazil and now lives in Ohio.

His interests include track, soccer, and helping build houses with Habitat for Humanity.

NEIL MUIR
New York
Student Argonaut, Mission 1

Neil has been fascinated with meteorology ever since Hurricane Frances hit Florida while he was there on vacation.

Neil serves as a peer mediator at school, conducting mediations with students in conflict.

ELLEN DRAKE
Ohio
Student Argonaut, Mission 1

Ellen is interested in pursuing a career in psychoanalysis.

Her hobbies include competitive swimming and classical piano.

CASSANDRA SANTAMARIA
California
Student Argonaut, Missions 4 and 5

Cassandra speaks Spanish, English, and French, and she spent five years living in Guaymas, Mexico.

Her hobbies include playing tennis and playing the violin.

JING FAN
Connecticut
Student Argonaut, Mission 3

Jing came to the United States from Beijing, China, when she was 10 years old.

She taught herself English in three years and now translates for visiting dignitaries.

AMANDA STUCKE
Oregon
Student Argonaut, Mission 3

Amanda runs track and practices dance five times each week.

She is considering a career as a physical therapist for dancers and athletes.

LAUREN GROSKAUFMANIS
Virginia
Student Argonaut, Missions 4 and 5

A Girl Scout since the first grade, Lauren earned the Bronze Award, the highest award a Junior Girl Scout can earn, and she is currently working on her Silver Award.

She has a keen interest in broadcasting and served as director for school TV shows.

MATTHEW WORSHAM
Ohio
Student Argonaut, Missions 4 and 5

Matthew is interested in paleotempestology, the study of hurricanes in the past.

He enjoys acting and recently played the role of Hector in the comedy "Here Comes the Judge."

CAMERON KING
Ohio
Student Argonaut, Mission 1

Cameron received his first chemistry set at age 10 and has been hooked on science ever since.

He engages in diverse activities, from being captain of his basketball team to breeding rabbits.

YOU ARE AN ARGONAUT TOO!

What are your interests? What would you want to tell other people about yourself? What do you like most about your JASON experience and being part of the JASON community?

Teacher Argonauts _____

CHRISTINE SILLS ARNOLD
Sigonella, Italy
Teacher Argonaut, Missions 4 and 5

Christine has 10 years of experience as a science teacher and currently teaches 7th grade at a DoDEA school in Sicily, Italy.

She grew up in Florida, where she became familiar with hurricanes up close.

DAWN BURBACH
Harlingen, TX
Teacher Argonaut, Mission 1

Dawn has taught 18 years and currently teaches K–5 gifted and talented students.

She believes that the key to being a JASON teacher is to think outside the box.

JOHN HARTMAN
Lakenheath, England
Teacher Argonaut, Mission 3

John was raised by hearing-impaired parents, an upbringing that helped him become an excellent communicator.

He serves as outdoor coordinator for the local Boy Scout troop where he sets up outdoor adventures, from 20-mile hikes to rock climbing and canoeing.

Argonaut Alumni _____

DANIELA AGUILERA
Maryland
Argonaut Alumnus, Mission 1

Daniela originally participated in *JASON XV: Rainforests at the Crossroads*, in Panama.

She plans to pursue a career in nursing.

JUSTINE PRUSS
New York
Argonaut Alumnus, Mission 3

Justine originally participated in *JASON XIII: Frozen Worlds,* in Alaska.

She credits JASON as the sole deciding factor for pursuing an education in biology.

ELIZABETH QUINTANA
Virginia
Argonaut Alumnus, Mission 2

Elizabeth originally participated in *JASON XV: Rainforests at the Crossroads*, in Panama.

She plans to pursue a career as a forensic scientist.

JEANETTE D. WILLIAMS-SMITH
Florida
Argonaut Alumnus, Missions 4 and 5

Jeanette was an Argonaut on *JASON X: Rainforests—A Wet & Wild Adventure.*

She received her B.S. degree in Biology from Eckerd College.

Host Researchers _____

ANTHONY GUILLORY
NASA's Wallops Flight Facility
Host Researcher, Mission 1

Anthony manages NASA's fleet of weather research planes.

He has participated in building weather stations for rural Alabama towns to help localize their weather forecasts.

ROBBIE HOOD
NASA's Wallops Flight Facility
Host Researcher, Mission 2

Robbie lived through one of the most devastating hurricanes of the 20th century, Hurricane Camille.

She has studied storms in and near Brazil, Alaska, and most recently the Cape Verde Islands.

TIM SAMARAS
National Geographic Emerging Explorer and Storm Chaser
Host Researcher, Mission 3

Tim became interested in tornadoes as a boy when he saw the motion picture *The Wizard of Oz.*

He also investigates lightning using high-speed film cameras.

JASON DUNION
NOAA's Hurricane Research Division
Host Researcher, Mission 4

Jason was a social worker before becoming a hurricane hunter.

He was inspired by the first NOAA satellite images used to show weather from space.

SHIRLEY MURILLO
NOAA's Hurricane Research Division
Host Researcher, Mission 5

Shirley lived through Hurricane Andrew in Miami and was motivated to learn more about hurricanes.

Her years of work with NOAA began with an internship during her senior year in high school.

Find out more about the team by going online: *www.jason.org*

Build a Barometer

Although you cannot see a change in air pressure, you can observe its effect on the surface of a stretched balloon skin. Here is how.

Materials
- wide-mouth glass jar
- large balloon
- scissors
- two drinking straws
- tape
- toothpick
- heavy stock paper
- metric ruler

Assembly

1. Stretch out a balloon by inflating and deflating it several times, then cut off the balloon's neck.

scale

2. Stretch the remaining balloon membrane over the mouth of the jar, forming a tight, flat, drum-like surface.

3. Insert one straw into another.

4. Tape a toothpick to one end of this length.

5. Tape the other end to the top of the jar at the center of the stretched membrane.

6. Draw a scale with 1-mm increments onto heavy stock paper and tape it to a vertical surface. Position the assembly so the toothpick pointer registers on the scale. Label this starting point as 0 on the scale. From that point, label every fifth mark above 0 in increments of 5. Label every fifth mark below 0 in increments of -5.

Calibrate the Barometer

7. Observe how changes in air pressure and weather affect the position of the pointer. Keep a daily log of these readings as you complete the *Monster Storms* curriculum.

Build a Wind Vane

Materials
- card stock
- drinking straw
- pin
- pencil
- directional compass
- scissors
- metric ruler

Assembly

1. Cut one small equilateral triangle from your card stock paper that is 2 cm (3/4 in.) long on each side. Also cut out a circle with a radius of about 3 cm (1 in.)

2. Cut two 2-cm-long slits directly opposite each other in one end of a drinking straw. Cut two 1-cm-long slits opposite each other in the other end of the straw.

3. Slide any side of the triangle into the 1-cm slits and the circle into the 2-cm slits in the straw. Push in both pieces until they are snug. This is the wind vane.

4. Place the wind vane on your finger to determine its balance point. Use a pin to anchor the straw into a pencil's eraser at the vane's balance point. Blow on the straw to make sure that it rotates freely. If it does not, make the holes in the straw slightly larger until it will rotate freely.

5. Use a directional compass to determine the orientation of the wind.

Build an Anemometer

Materials
- tape
- foam packing peanut
- protractor with hole at measurement vertex
- paper clip
- straw
- fan

Assembly

1. Use a piece of tape to attach a foam packing peanut to one end of a drinking straw.

2. Bend open a paper clip so that it has an "S" shape.

3. Poke the paper clip through the side of the straw, and then loop the clip through the vertex hole in the protractor. The paper clip should act like a chain link that allows the straw to swing freely at this pivot point on the protractor.

Calibrate the Anemometer

4. Stand 1 m (3 ft) directly in front of a 3-speed fan on a table. Have another student turn the speed up from low speed, to medium speed, to high speed.

5. Hold your anemometer with the straight edge of the protractor in a horizontal position as shown, so that when the straw is at rest, it measures an angle of 90 degrees.

6. Record the maximum angle measured at each speed. This will be the difference between 90 degrees and your reading on the protractor. This is your wind speed scale.

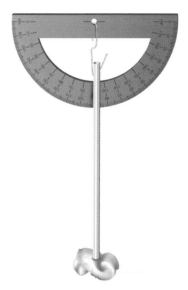

Build a Rain Gauge

Materials
- clear, flat-bottom vial with same diameter from the bottom to the mouth
- permanent marker
- metric ruler

Assembly

1. At 1-cm intervals, mark off the depth of the vial, starting from the bottom.

2. Place the vial in an open location to collect precipitation.

Build a Hair Hygrometer

Materials
- shoebox
- 3 in. x 5 in. note card
- pin
- strands of hair at least 25 cm (10 in.) long
- tape
- metric ruler

Assembly

1. Cut a 3 in. x 5 in. note card into a triangular pointer, as shown in the apparatus below.

2. Tape a dime or item of similar mass on the centerline of the pointer, about halfway between its middle and its pointed end, as shown.

3. Use a push pin or brad to anchor the widest end of the pointer at the bottom of the back of the shoebox. Be careful not to stick yourself with the push pin!

4. Draw measurement marks along the arc of the path traced out by the end of the pointer at 0.5-cm intervals, as shown.

5. Tape one end of the hair strands to the bottom edge of the pointer, as shown.

6. Extend the hair strands up so that the hair is taut and the pointer is horizontal. Tape the other end of the hair strands to the upper portion of the shoebox, as shown.

Calibrate the Hygrometer

7. Wet a piece of paper towel with warm water.

8. Dab the hair strands with the paper towel.

9. Stand the shoebox upright and tape the box to your table. Mark the position of the pointer for this high-humidity measurement. Label it "High H." (You may want to make this measurement by using hot water, which will make it more humid.)

10. Dry the hair strands with a hair dryer. Mark the position of the pointer for this low-humidity measurement. Label it "Low H."

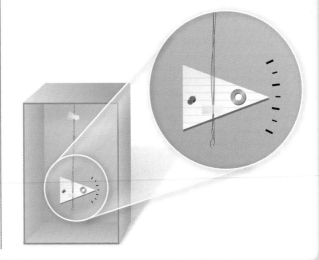

Build a Dew Point Tool

Materials
- metal can (1 liter or larger)
- water
- stir stick
- ice
- thermometer

Assembly

1. Read the thermometer and record the air temperature.

2. Fill the can about halfway with water and allow the temperature of the water to reach equilibrium with the air temperature.

3. Add ice to the water and stir with the stir stick. Do not use the thermometer to stir the ice water!

4. Observe the sides of the can and watch for condensation to appear.

5. Record the temperature of the water when condensation first forms on the outside of the can. This is the dew point temperature.

Glossary

A

absolute humidity a measure of the mass of water vapor in a volume of air (40)

air pressure the pressure exerted in every direction by the air (14)

atmosphere the layers of gases that surround Earth, which include the troposphere, stratosphere, mesosphere, and thermosphere (8, 29)

B

blizzard a severe winter storm characterized by strong winds and heavy snow. A winter storm is classified as a blizzard when it reduces visibility to 0.4 km (1/4 mi) or less for three or more consecutive hours, and has wind speeds of at least 56 km/h (35 mph). (9, 100)

C

climate the average condition of the weather in a region over a period of years, as described by its range of temperature, winds, humidity, and precipitation (13)

condensation a change of state from gas to liquid, caused by the loss of heat energy in the gas (31, 33)

conduction the transfer of heat energy between atoms and molecules that occurs within an object or between objects that touch (19)

convection the transfer of heat energy that occurs by the flow of material (19, 20, 73)

Coriolis Effect the spiraling of winds produced by Earth's rotation. In the Northern Hemisphere, tropical storms spiral in a counterclockwise direction, whereas in the Southern Hemisphere they spiral in a clockwise direction. Generally, the farther from the equator a storm is positioned, the more the Coriolis Effect will influence the rotation of the storm. (71)

cyclone the term used for a tropical cyclone that forms in the Indian Ocean or South Pacific Ocean (71, 75)

D

density a measure of mass per unit volume (28)

deposition the process by which snow and frost form when water vapor changes directly to a solid state (31)

dew moisture that has condensed on objects near the ground, whose temperatures have fallen below the dew point temperature (39)

dew point the temperature at which water vapor begins to condense into liquid water (40, 41, 51, 64)

Doppler radar enhanced radar that can detect storm location, intensity and amount of precipitation, wind speed and direction toward and away from the radar site, rotational patterns in wind, and other valuable weather data (60, 72, 81)

dropsonde a weather detection device designed to be dropped from a hurricane hunter aircraft to collect data on tropical storm conditions as the device falls to Earth. It collects data on global position, air pressure, temperature, humidity, wind speed, and wind direction. It typically relays the data to a computer in the airplane by radio transmission. (81, 89)

drought a prolonged period of below-normal rainfall over a large geographic area, with severe effects, including a shortage of fresh water for consumption, crop loss, and wildfires (10, 102)

dry line a boundary at which moist air meets dry air (52, 58, 64)

E

EF-Scale the Enhanced Fujita Scale, used to classify tornadoes, is expanded from the original Fujita Scale to include more diverse and more descriptive physical damage indicators (57, 89)

electromagnetic spectrum a system that classifies the different forms of electromagnetic radiation according to wavelength (12)

evaporation a change of state from liquid to gas, caused by the gain of heat energy in the liquid (31, 32)

eye circular region located at the center of a hurricane. The eye usually has calm weather. (71)

eyewall region of tall clouds, heavy rain, and strong winds surrounding a hurricane's eye. The eyewall is where the most severe rain and winds of a hurricane occur. (71, 88–89)

F

flood any unusually high flow, overflow, or inundation by water that causes or threatens to cause damage. (10, 103)

fog water droplets suspended in the air at Earth's surface. Fog is often hazardous when it reduces visibility to 0.4 km (1/4 mile) or less. (39)

freezing a transformation or phase change from liquid to solid (**31**)

front a boundary or transition zone between two air masses of different density, and thus (usually) of different temperature. A moving front is named according to the advancing air mass; e.g., cold front if colder air is advancing. (**52**, 62)

frost the deposition of water vapor as thin ice crystals on the ground or other surfaces. Frost forms under conditions similar to those that cause dew, except that the temperatures of Earth's surface and of earthbound objects falls below the freezing point temperature of 0°C (32°F). (**39**)

Fujita Scale a scale ranging from F0 (least intense) to F5 (most intense), used to classify tornadoes according to wind speed and the damage that can occur (**57**)

───────────── **G** ─────────────

global warming an overall increase in world temperatures that may be caused by additional heat being trapped by greenhouse gases (**13**)

greenhouse effect the natural reuse and retention of atmospheric heat, which helps warm the planet. Certain heat-retaining gases, such as water vapor, carbon dioxide, methane, and ozone, are the primary molecules that retain this heat in the air. (**13**)

───────────── **H** ─────────────

hail a form of precipitation produced by cumulonimbus clouds and characterized by balls or irregular lumps of ice (hailstones) about 5–50 mm (0.2–2.0 in.) in diameter on average (**9**)

heat wave a period of abnormally, uncomfortably, and even dangerously hot and humid weather. In North America, a heat wave is usually defined as three or more consecutive days with temperatures over 32.2°C (90°F). (**10**)

humidity a measure of the water vapor content of the air. The higher the temperature, the greater the amount of water the air can maintain in a vapor state. (31, **40**)

hurricane the term used for a tropical cyclone that forms over warm ocean water in the North Atlantic or eastern North Pacific. A tropical storm becomes a hurricane when its sustained winds reach a speed of 119 km/h (74 mph). (**8**, 71, 72, 74–75)

───────────── **I** ─────────────

isobars lines connecting points of equal air pressure on a weather map (**62**)

───────────── **K** ─────────────

kinetic energy the energy possessed by a moving body of matter as a result of its motion (**50**)

knot a unit of speed equal to one nautical mile per hour, or 1.15 statute (regular) miles per hour. (22, **89**)

───────────── **L** ─────────────

latent heat energy heat released or absorbed by a substance during a phase change (**13**, **50**)

lightning the emission of visible light during a powerful natural electrostatic discharge, produced during a thunderstorm, that returns electrical stability to the air. This abrupt electric discharge is accompanied by a shock wave produced by the explosive expansion of heated air (thunder). (**9**, 54, 99, 100, **106–107**)

───────────── **M** ─────────────

melting a transformation or phase change from solid to liquid (**31**)

───────────── **P** ─────────────

phase change any change in a solid, liquid, or gas to another physical state. A phase change involves the transfer of energy but not a change in chemical composition. (**31**, 36)

───────────── **R** ─────────────

radiation transfer of energy that occurs by the propagation of electromagnetic waves (**19**)

rainbands regions of heavy thunderstorms beyond the eyewall that spiral outward from the center of a hurricane (**71**)

relative humidity a ratio comparing the amount of water vapor in the air with the total amount of water vapor that the air can maintain at that temperature (**40**)

runoff precipitation that is not absorbed by the ground and instead flows downhill to low-lying areas and into rivers and streams. Severe runoff can cause floods and flash floods. (**10**, 99)

Saffir-Simpson Scale a ranking of Category 1 to Category 5, that is used to classify hurricanes according to wind speed and the amount of damage that could occur (**89**, 90, 92)

Saharan Air Layer a hot, dry, dusty air layer that forms over North Africa in the summer and affects the formation of hurricanes in the Atlantic Ocean (**78**)

sensible heat heat emitted by Earth's surface and absorbed by the surrounding atmosphere (**13**)

storm a violent weather event such as a hurricane, thunderstorm, or blizzard (**8**)

storm surge a large wave of water that is pushed onshore by wind. During a hurricane, the storm surge is what typically poses the greatest threat to life and property. (**89**, 92, 94)

stratosphere the layer of Earth's atmosphere above the troposphere. The stratosphere begins about 11 km (7 mi) above Earth and ends about 50 km (31 mi) above Earth. Clouds rarely form here, and the air is very cold and thin. (**29**, 30, 31)

sublimation a transformation or phase change from solid to gas (**31**)

supercell the largest, strongest, most hazardous type of thunderstorm, having a strong zone of rotation. Supercells are capable of producing tornadoes, hail, torrential rain, and dangerous bursts of wind. (**8**, 56)

temperature inversion a condition of the atmosphere during which a layer of warmer, less dense air lies above a layer of cooler, denser air (**78**)

thunder the sonic boom (produced by the violent expansion of super-heated air) that occurs when a lightning bolt discharges during an electrical storm (**54**)

thunderstorm a storm having thunder and lightning, usually having strong wind and heavy rain and sometimes having hail or tornadoes that form as warm, moist air rises (**8**, 50, 99)

tornado a violently spinning column of air extending down from a thunderstorm and in contact with the ground (**8**, 56, 79, 98)

Tornado Alley a region through the Great Plains of the Central United States where conditions are particularly favorable for tornado development (**58**)

tropical cyclone massive tropical storm that forms over warm ocean water, with extremely strong winds spiraling around a center of low air pressure (**71**, 75)

troposphere the lowest layer of the atmosphere where almost all weather occurs. The troposphere contains about 80% of the atmosphere's mass and is characterized by temperatures that normally decrease with altitude. The boundary between the troposphere and the stratosphere depends on latitude and season. It ranges from as low as 8 km (5 mi) over the poles to as high as 16–18 km (9.9–11.1 mi) in the tropics. (**29**, 30, 31, 51)

typhoon the term used for a tropical cyclone that forms in the Pacific Ocean near Asia (**71**, 75)

warning generally, an alert issued when severe weather is in progress. In the U.S., the National Weather Service issues severe storm warnings on a per county basis. (**96**)

watch generally, an alert issued by the National Weather Service when conditions are favorable for severe weather to develop (**96**)

water cycle the continuous circulation of water within Earth's atmosphere, land, surface water, and groundwater. The process is driven by solar radiation. As water moves through the cycle, it changes state among liquid, solid, and gaseous states. (**32**, 33, 34)

water vapor the colorless, odorless, invisible, gaseous form of water in the atmosphere (**32**, 37, **50**, 72)

wavelength the distance between adjacent peaks in a series of periodic waves (**12**)

weather a state of the atmosphere that is often described by measured values of weather variables, such as pressure, precipitation, and humidity (**8**)

wind the perceptible movement of air from an area of higher air pressure to an area of lower air pressure (**15**)

wind barb a symbol used in reporting meteorological observations of wind speed and direction. The shaft indicates the direction from which the wind is coming; on the shaft, each half-barb represents a wind speed of 5 knots, each full barb is 10 knots, and each flag is 50 knots. (**22**, 63, 82-83)

wind shear a change in wind speed and/or direction at different heights in the atmosphere (**72**, 73, 78)

Credits

The JASON Project would like to acknowledge the many people who have made valuable contributions in the development of the *Operation: Monster Storms* curriculum.